ISBN 978-1-332-34497-0
PIBN 10316795

This book is a reproduction of an important historical work. Forgotten Books uses
state-of-the-art technology to digitally reconstruct the work, preserving the original format
whilst repairing imperfections present in the aged copy. In rare cases, an imperfection in
the original, such as a blemish or missing page, may be replicated in our edition. We do,
however, repair the vast majority of imperfections successfully; any imperfections that
remain are intentionally left to preserve the state of such historical works.

English
Français
Deutsche
Italiano
Español
Português

www.forgottenbooks.com

Mythology Photography **Fiction**
Fishing Christianity **Art** Cooking
Essays Buddhism Freemasonry
Medicine **Biology** Music **Ancient
Egypt** Evolution Carpentry Physics
Dance Geology **Mathematics** Fitness
Shakespeare **Folklore** Yoga Marketing
Confidence Immortality Biographies
Poetry **Psychology** Witchcraft
Electronics Chemistry History **Law**
Accounting **Philosophy** Anthropology
Alchemy Drama Quantum Mechanics
Atheism Sexual Health **Ancient History**
Entrepreneurship Languages Sport
Paleontology Needlework Islam
Metaphysics Investment Archaeology
Parenting Statistics Criminology
Motivational

In the Bosom of the Comanches

A Thrilling Tale of Savage Indian Life, Massacre
and Captivity Truthfully Told by
a Surviving Captive

Texas Borderland Perils and Scenes Depicted

The Closing Days of the Trying Indian Struggles
upon the Frontiers of Texas

By
T. A. BABB
Amarillo, Texas

PRESS OF
JOHN F. WORLEY PRINTING CO.
DALLAS

$1.50

©CI.A328866

no 1

DOT BABB

Index to Illustrations

INTRODUCTION

In the unchallenged verity of the chronicle of Theodore Adolphus Babb, better known as Dot Babb, recorded in the pages that follow is vouchsafed a sustained and absorbing interest to the reader and the student: a dissolvent of the mystical haziness that has characterized so much of the Indian lore, current hitherto; and a contribution to history, an inestimable legacy and gift to posterity as rare and timely as truth is mighty and eternal. Mr. Babb, a descendant of resolute venturesome pioneer stock, entered upon an eventful boyhood in the untamed wilds of the western border of Texas in a locality and period when the mounted Indian marauder with his panoply of war and death was often seen silhouetted against the distant horizon, at a time when the spectre of tragedy and desolation, of atrocious massacre, mutilation, captivity, and torture, cast its terrifying shadow athwart the fireside of every pioneer home; when, unheralded, cunning monsters of vindictive savage hate, here and there among the settlers, in unguarded repose or fancied security, sprang from stealthy ambush, from the wood-lands' dark border, the sheltering hillside and gulch, or the shadowy lustre of an unwelcome fateful full moon, and amid and unheeding the shrieks of horror, and frenzied slaughter, mingled with the cries of anguish and prayers of women and children kneeling before their doom, they struck with the fangs of the most vicious, merciless, and unreasoning beast, and in their unrestrained and unresisted madness and ferocity, they left in their crimson wake a sickening chapter of ghastly human wreckage of whole families exterminated, in either a fiendish butchery or revolting captivity without a counterpart in all the annals of every race and age since the hour of the dawn of Christendom, if not since the world began.

At a time when there were no white flags and no surrender, and only such alternatives as death, flight, or captivity; when lion-hearted men defiant of frightful consequences went afield, tended the herds and flocks, and pursued the chase and all the vocations of daily life heavily armed, perhaps never to return, or returning to find a home in ruin and the family either annihilated or some members murdered, some made captive, and still others that miraculously escaped by flight, concealment, the coincidence of absence, or being stricken down and unwittingly left for dead; when upon these scenes of appalling desolation men and women assembled, the survivors buried their dead and with the gory fragments builded again, animated by the one unconquerable purpose to defend, hold, or die on their border heritage. At a time when keenest vigil day and night was never relaxed by man or beast, when the horizon was anxiously scanned for the ascending camp fire smoke, swirling clouds of dust or other such unfailing portents of the red messengers of devastation and death; when every moonbeam and shadow in thicket or grove, when every sound or noise breaking the slumbrous solitudes (whether a gust of wind or the flapping of wings or plaintive notes of nocturnal fowls) was seen, heard, and interpreted with strained senses of preternatural power; at a time when swift hoofbeats rang out upon the stillness of the night the warning of perhaps the sole survivor of the latest massacre, and, with relays of horses fleeting and untiring as if conscious of their mission, the gruesome tidings were borne to the settler far and near. Being thus warned Spartan men and women grimly and silently prepared for the onslaught, padlocking corrals, replenishing the supply of water from the spring or well, barricading doors and with shotted rifles, bullet molds, and powder, stoically awaited the attack. During the nerve-racking watches of the dismal night, as babes and children lapsed into a slumber perhaps eternal, no sentinel nodded or slept at his expectant post. When at length the attack came, the defenders, conscious that no quarter could be asked or given, were transformed into an incarnation of billegerent fury, a super-human maelstrom of action and combative power, and with souls and all reserve forces and energies ablaze, and an unconquerable purpose to shield and preserve their loved ones, they grappled with the demoniacal savage. Failing, all perished together upon the hallowed altar and sanctuary of a family and home pulsating and resounding a few hours before with emotions and manifestations of love, joy, and hope.

From this crucible of dramatic episodes, struggle, and peril, Dot Babb was evolved, and amid such stirring scenes he passed his early youth and advancing boyhood up to the hour of the tragical climax of the unutterably horrifying and heartrending spectacle of his beloved mother impaled by the Indians as she pleaded for her children and his still deeper sorrow in being torn from her dying embrace for the inevitable captivity which immediately followed and her farewell words of solace in his inconsolable distress, and the tender maternal benediction gently spoken as he looked back into tear bedewed eyes for the last glimpse and vision on earth of a sainted face on which he plainly saw the unmistakable pallor of fast approaching death. In his enforced captivity by the Comanches, one of the fiercest Indian tribes then extant, Dot Babb approached his maturing years as a full-fledged warrior, being made to engage in raids and battles in common with the Indian braves. His experiences, privations, and exploits he recounts with the simplicity and vividness of truth, and in a like manner details his reclamation by the United States Army and his eventual restoration to the fragmentary units of his shattered family, his recivilization and subsequent career notable for the highest probity of character and usefulness as a most worthy and valued citizen down to this good hour, which finds him happy and prosperous in the sunset of a thrilling life, whether peacefully pursuing the herds on the broad acres of his Panhandle ranch or extending the proverbial pioneer hospitality of a spacious and beautiful home in Amarillo, Texas, to his old-time friends, who are legion. Upon his return from an unwilling militant service in the ranks of the red warriors to the society of his fellows, Mr. Babb was quick to re-adopt and experience a complete revival of the inherent sentiments and amenities of civilized life. After becoming settled in his chosen avocation of cattle raising he married the splendid and estimable woman who to-day is his greatest comfort in presiding over his elegant and hospitable home and in sharing with him the honor and blessing of the sterling family they have reared.

At an impressionable age Dot Babb, the boy captive and warrior, had much intimate contact with the inner Indian life, motives, habits and tribal laws, superstitions, joys, and sorrows, of which the Dot Babb of to-day discloses glimpses as rare as they are interesting and instructive. Mr. Babb found much worthy of admiration and emulation if not adoption in the Indian character, in their traditional laws, heroic and domestic life; and being made familiar with the Indian view point he has found no little to condone and defend that in the public imagination has had universal and popular condemnation. In the period of his captivity there were cemented between him and many of the chiefs and the rank and file ties of strongest attachment that have not waned in all the lapse of time. Not a few of the ex-warriors now dwelling in comfort and contentment upon their allotments learned long ago after a fashion to write a mixed Indian and English dialect and have persevered in an unbroken correspondence throughout all the intervening years with Mr. Babb, who both speaks and writes the Indian language with the fluency and ease of a Comanche.

It has also been a fixed custom of Mr. Babb to make visits at regular intervals to many of his old surviving captors, and is received and entertained by them with an almost unexampled joy and hospitality and perhaps more so than if he were one of their tribal kin and brethren. In fact the Comanches have all along regarded him as the son of their rightful adoption and when the big Fort Sill reservation was being made ready for allotment and settlement Mr. Babb was urged by Chief Quanah Parker and subordinates to qualify for allotments for himself and each member of his family in common with the Comanche and Kiowa Indians. In all their dealings with the United States government and in all important tribal questions and affairs, whether business, domestic, or social, the counsel and advice of Mr. Babb has been sought and freely given, as he has ever been their steadfast friend and co-worker. In their relations there have been the same mutual confidence and reciprocal esteem and sympathy that obtain in the better forms of civilized society.

Mr. Babb is therefore doubly unique in his dual adaptability to Indian life and tradition and to the best business and social life as found in the higher circles of substantial, refined, and enlightened men and women. It can hardly be said that any man living to-day is equipped with the same experience, observation, and knowledge and can speak so authoritatively of the Indian era of Texas, the old Indian Territory, and the Southwest as Mr. Babb. Therefore the narrative of Mr. Babb, replete with deepest human interest and much pathos, and descriptive of expeditions of war and savage fury, as well as of the latter life of the subdued Indian, with his crimson tomahawk discarded forever, is the truest link yet formed between the Indian and civilization. As the Indian, America's first great settler, with such biographers and interpreters of his life, exploits, and character as Mr. Babb, is now essaying his role in the closing scene of the last contemporaneous drama, Mr. Babb's realistic portrayal, is nothing short of a noteworthy contribution to the best Indian archives and an ampler appreciation of one of the stirring epochs of a nation; and as such it is dedicated to the entertainment and edification of the generations of to-day and those to follow.

ALBERT SIDNEY STINNETT,
Editor and Biographer.

JAMES W. BABB, Dot Babb's Grandfather

Dot Babb and his horse Old Coley.

In the Bosom of the Comanches

My name is Theodore Adolphus Babb, better known as Dot Babb. I was born May 17th, 1852, near Reedsburg in Saurk County, Wisconsin, to which place my father emigrated from Ohio in an early day. In 1854 my father with his family consisting of my mother and brother, Hernandez Cortez Babb and myself, entered upon the long journey to Texas. We traveled the entire distance in a two-horse wagon, and were twelve months on the road. Our first stop in Texas was in Grayson county near Sherman. About one year later our family moved in ox wagons to what was known as Dry creek in Wise county, about twelve miles west of Decatur, Texas. My earliest definite recollections were in our new home on Dry creek. There were but few white people in that section at that time, but the Indians were numerous. These Indians were then friendly, and remained so till fugitive outlaws and renegades from other states commenced killing and stealing their ponies, and also killing the Indians who undertook to recover their ponies. The Indians at length decided to strike back, and putting all the white people in the same class commenced their depredations upon the white settlers generally about the time of the breaking out of the civil war. This caused the state of Texas to place its rangers on the western border from the Indian Territory to Mexico, and ample protection was afforded up to the close of the war between the states, at which time the southern soldier was disarmed and the state government turned over to an alien militia concentrated at the state capital and other centers of population. The border settlers had but little if any protection from that time and the Indians became cruelly savage, killing and scalping whole families, taking children into captivity, stealing horses, and engaging in all manner of barbaric practices and deeds.

In the spring of 1865 my father, Jno. S. Babb, and my older brother, H. C. Babb, started out with a drove of cattle for the markets of Arkansas, leaving mother, me, and two sisters at home. My oldest sister was nine years old, my baby sister eleven months, and I about thirteen years old. There was also making her home with us a Mrs. Luster, about twenty-two years old, whose husband was killed in the Civil War. There were two other families living on our place, and all were within three or four hundred yards of each other. One of the families, Harbolt by name, had several boys, some of whom became notorious outlaws in later years, and many old timers will recall the name of Jim Harbolt as a terrible bandit of the darkest days of the Indian Territory.

The other family was that of the widow Estes and her several children.

About the middle of September, 1865, between three and four o'clock in the afternoon, my eldest sister and I were at play when we discovered thirty-five or forty Comanche Indians in all the regalia and war paint of the savage warrior. Stupified with fright we looked again and realized that they were advancing rapidly upon us, and with quickened heart-beats we wondered what our fate would be at the hands of these emissaries of murderous implacable hate. We soon saw they would raid our home, and with their weird and unearthly war whoops ringing in our ears we ran to the house for the protection of mother and Mrs. Luster, who had also seen and heard the demons approaching. Mother had us enter the house as quickly as possible and closed the unbarricaded doors. It would be indeed impossible to describe the emotions of horror that possessed all of us in this moment of fatal doom and peril. There was no time for either lamentation or prayer with our helplessness accentuated by the lack of every means of defense; and justifiable premonitions of death were proclaimed in our tremulous voices and fear-distorted faces. An eternity of horror crowded into a moment of insufferable suspense for unprotected and undefended women and children, confronted by merciless and remorseless savages whose known acts and lives were records of treachery and blood.

Mrs. Luster undertook to conceal herself in the loft of the log cabin and I made for two or three old guns in their racks on the wall. Simultaneously several of the Indians

JOHN S. BABB
Father of Dot Babb. Born 1810, Died 1880.

broke open the door and as I would seize a gun they would take it from me and belabor me over the head with their quirts. My mother was trying to soften or make friends by shaking hands with them, and against these overtures they were as surlily obdurate and unmoved as ever these ruthless slayers had been painted. The first thing in their diabolical performances was to plunder our home and take off everyting in the way of clothing and bedding. They then had Mrs. Luster come down from her hiding in the loft and she was bound by some Indians and taken outside to the other Indians and their horses and there declared a captive. The remainder of the Indians in the house seized my oldest sister and started off with her. My mother, prompted by an uncontrollable maternal instinct and affection, interfered and clung to my sister in an effort to prevent her being taken, and as she did so one of the Indians stabbed my mother four times with a big butcher knife. They then took my sister from the house and made captive of her also, along with Mrs. Luster. Seeing my mother brutally and fatally stabbed I assisted her to the bed just as two of the Indians came back, and not finding my mother dead as they expected, one of them with drawn bow shot her in the left side with an arrow that ranged up towards her lungs. I pulled the arrow out and sat upon the bed by her, doing all I could to console and comfort her as her strength and life waned. The same Indian drew his bow and pointed a deadly arrow at me and commanded me to go with him. Mother, seeing that I too would be killed if I resisted or refused, said, "Go with him and be a good boy." One of them then grabbed me by the arm and jerked me off the bed, and as he dragged me towards the door the other Indian pounded me with his quirt. In this miserable plight I was forcibly separated from my mother, dying in a mass of blood, with my baby sister enclasped within her arms.

OMERCAWBEY (Walking Face) Nephew of Chief Horse Back

A very desperate Indian who shot my mother with arrows at the time she was killed and I captured. I never saw him afterwards, but understood later that he had been shot to death.—Dot Babb

Here in a time of trustful security, as the light laughter of playing children mingled with the songs of birds, and love and joy unconfined rioted in the fondest and most sacred family ties, in a few terrible moments was written in blood a chapter of human bitterness and sorrow at which all civilization and mankind would stand aghast. A home rent asunder, a mother sacrificed in anguishing torture and death upon the altar of dutiful devotion and purposeful life, a young woman and a youthful son and daughter torn from the family roof-tree to be carried into the unknown wilds and the forbidding and darkest realms of the fiercest and most unrelenting savage barbarians that ever trod the earth, an unrestrained, inhuman, savage debauchery crying aloud for the intervention and mercies of God and man.

When they got outside with me I saw my sister and Mrs. Luster mounted on horses, each with an Indian in front of her on the same horse, thus riding in double fashion. I was placed on a horse in a similar manner, with my hands tightly held by my Indian riding mate. The plunder taken from my home had been securely fastened on the pack animals, and with the three captives, consisting of my sister, Mrs. Luster, and myself, the cavalcade, without ceremony but with much solemnity, fear, and sorrow upon the part of the captives, hastily moved off the premises. When we had gone about half a mile we came upon several of my father's horses grazing upon the common. The Indians selected some of the younger of these horses, which they drove along with the other horses they had seized or stolen and then took a route up Dry creek right through where the town of Chico is now located, thence northwest, pushing onward after nightfall and only stopping two or three times the entire night for short intervals of rest. By nine o'clock the next morning we were out of the cross timbers and into an open plains country. Fearing pursuit it was a custom of the Indians

BLACK HAWK AND SQUAW.
evere Fighter in the Indian Davs

returning from a raid with captives, stolen horses, and other booty to undergo fatigue, hunger, and all manner of privation and to exert themselves and horses to the point of exhaustion to get beyond the line the white settlers would venture to follow. Therefore, for many hours the Indians gave us but little rest and neither food nor sleep, but pressed onward persistently and swiftly.

We at length reached the Little Wichita river, which was swollen by recent floods to brimming bank full; but the Indians found a big accumulation of drift, on which we crossed dismounted, the horses being made to swim the river. The first thing we had to eat during the many hours since setting out on this unwilling, mournful journey was after we had crossed the Little Wichita river and reached Holiday creek, about eighteen miles southwest from the site of the present city of Wichita Falls. This feast was on the remains of a big steer that the lobo wolves had freshly slain and of which they had eaten both hams as was their custom. From here we proceeded to the Big Wichita river which we crossed just below the mouth of Beaver creek, and this course was kept till we reached Red river that afternoon about sunset at a point a little below the mouth of Pease river. Being now comparatively safe from pursuit, the Indians halted with us for three days and four nights, and during the time they took rest and also nursed a wounded Indian who had been shot with a bullet through the right knee in a skirmish that they had with settlers before they reached and devastated our home. In this particular raid they encountered stubborn resistance and had four or five severe fights up to the time of attacking our lamented home and family. In the first of these fights they killed two white men and two negroes on Carrol's creek, south of Jacksboro, Texas, and in the fights that followed with the Owens, Higgins, and Armstrongs, they had slain four of their warriors, but they managed to carry off three of their dead and only left one to be scalped by the whites.

The next fight was with Ben Blanton, Glen Halsell and Lansing Hunt. These men were working for Dan Waggoner, and had penned some cattle that they might brand the calves at the old Thorn place about three miles southeast of our home. There was a family living on the old Thorn place by the name of Couch, but the man or head of the family was not at home and the three men were busy branding out in the corrals when the Indians charged them. The men ran to the house where Mrs. Couch and two little children were and prepared for a stubborn defence. The Indians attacked fiercely and time and again were driven back by the deadly aim of the three men besieged in the house. The Indians, after having two of their number killed and one wounded in the knee became discouraged and withdrew, taking with them several horses and bridles and also their dead. According to Indian superstition there would be direful consequences if they failed to carry their dead off the battlefield, and this they never failed to do unless in unpreventable and exceptional cases. Their next attack was upon our home and in manner and results previously detailed.

Resuming the course of the flight of the Indians with their captives and loot, following the three days rest with the wounded Indian on the south bank of Red river, they crossed Red river, taking a northwesterly course and crossing the North Fork of the Red river at the mouth of Stinking creek in what is now known as Greer county, Oklahoma. Continuing they went by Headquarters mountain and stayed all night, and next morning we crossed North fork again and thus gained the northeast side of that stream and kept a northwest course until we stopped on the Washita river the next night. Keeping a northwesterly course we reached the Canadian river at the end of another hard day's travel, and on its banks they pitched their camp for the night. Here in the night's repose Mrs. Luster and I made our first desperate attempt at escape from captivity. Mrs. Luster laid the plans and directed me during the day to be sure and fasten a certain fine horse so he could not get far away and that there was a mare that would stay with him. These two animals were stolen on this raid from our neighbors the Owens. I secured the knot of the rope on this horse between two limbs. In making the beds for the night they made one which they had Mrs. Luster, sister, and me occupy, and the Indians then slept all around us. I was so tired I went to sleep and did not wake till Mrs. Luster nudged me into wakefulness about one o'clock in the morning. The moon in the east was two hours high and the Indians all were sleeping soundly.

We realized we were about to embark upon a perilous undertaking, but in our desperation we were quite re-signed to the consequences. As I viewed these savages, asleep and contemplated the cruel faces half lighted by the moon's rays that filtered through the leaves of the trees, the scene and the predicament thrilled me with a sense of indescribable horror. Mrs. Luster and I stole noiselessly away from our bunk upon the ground and with cat-like stealth tiptoed to the horses. Mrs. Luster found a bridle and this we put on the horse previously secured and led him to a log from which she could mount. Mrs. Luster then whispered to me to get a bridle for the mare I was to ride. I got the bridle but the Indians awoke before I could get the bridle on the mare and came running towards us. Meantime Mrs. Luster had mounted and I told her to get away if she could, whereupon she bade me good-bye and with the stillness and swiftness of a shadow disappeared into the night. I threw the bridle away and turned back and in this way for the time being disarmed the suspicion of the Indians who had been aroused and noting my absence started in pursuit. Upon returning I laid down and could sleep no more for thinking

BLACK HAWK, Old-Time Indian Warrior.

and wondering what they would do to me for trying to escape and it seemed an age before day dawned once more.

It was fully an hour after my return before they discovered that Mrs. Luster had escaped and then eight or ten Indians entered excitedly upon her pursuit. At length daylight came and all the Indians got up and the ones who had gone on a fruitless search for Mrs. Luster came back. They waked my little sister and had her get up and then all formed a line and one of them took and stood me against a big cotton wood tree. They took their bows and arrows and some old cap and ball pistols and were in line some twenty or thirty yards from me and the one who had conducted me to the tree made signs to me that they were going to riddle me with bullets and arrows and then take my scalp and have a big war dance over it. Here again my whole past life came into instant review and in the procession of events that quickly passed were visions of kindred, boyhood scenes of joy and sorrow and the woful and pathetic face of my lamented mother, stricken and dying from the deadly knife-thrusts and arrows of my fiendish captors. My little nine-year-old sister being made to look on the line of warriors with guns and bows and arrows trained on me burst forth into paroxysms of wailing cries, and sobbings. In this moment of doom I spoke to her in quieting, endearing terms, and when she thought the next instant would be my last she fell upon the ground and hid her face. I was sure they were going to kill me, and wanting the scene closed I made signs to them to shoot and end my unbearable suspense. When I did this, several of the Indians relaxed their drawn weapons and thrust themselves between me and the line of executioners; and then all the Indians came up and pushed the impulsive defenders aside and took a raw-hide rope and tied me to the tree. They then pulled long dead grass and collected a lot of dry brush from the nearby trees and placed all around

MRS. J. D. BELL, Sister of Dot Babb.

Taken into captivity by the Comanche Indians with Dot, as related in this book.
Mrs. Bell, with her husband and six children, resides at Denton, Texas.

me, preparatory to cremating me alive, and during all this time my sister's cries broke the solitudes of these savage wilds. They had no matches, but used flint and steel in making fires; and the flint and steel they placed by the grass and brush piled about and over me, and then held what seemed a last council. Being more than ever tired of these preliminaries I made signs to them to fire the grass, but instead of doing so they all came forward saying, "Heap wano you," and untied me.

I afterwards learned from them that my seeming total lack of fear and utter defiance of the most painful of deaths evidenced the qualities and courage needful in a warrior, and as such they spared my life and attached or adopted me as a prospective militant tribesman. Seeing

---

Nov. 28, 1911.

Mr. A. S. Stinnett.

Your letter of recent date has not been answered promptly on account of my absence as a delegate to the Peace Conference in Rome, Italy. I knew the Babb family well in Wise County many years ago, and I introduced and now have pending in the House of Representatives a bill to refund to them the value of the property destroyed, burned and carried away by the Comanche Indians when Dot Babb, then a boy, and his sister Bianca, were captured and carried off by the Indians, and their home burned and part of the family killed, etc. I have never been able to get this bill through because there are hundreds of similar cases and this bill, if passed, would open the door for all similar cases. I have also a general bill now pending in Congress that would cover this and all similar cases, by permitting the claimant to bring suit in the Court of Claims against the U. S. Government, for the value of their property; and hope to get it through at the coming session of Congress. Bianca Babb (one of the prisoners) is now the wife of Mr. J. D. Bell, of Denton, Texas, and the claim of Dot Babb and herself has been fully proven by affidavits filed by me with the Committee on Indian Affairs (of which I am now the chairman), and I have no doubt of their justice or the truth of their statements, and I shall do everything in my power to aid them in recovering the value of the property destroyed, etc., but not for their personal injuries or imprisonment or for the death of other members of the family. as there is no precedent for such action of Congress, and at this late date it would be utterly useless to ask for such damages.

Yours very truly,

JNO. H. STEPHENS.

CONGRESSMAN JOHN H. STEPHENS

the pall of death lifted from me, my little sister embraced me and wept for joy. The next step was to take up the trail and recapture Mrs. Luster, in whose escape the previous night I had assisted, for which I so nearly forfeited my life. Mrs. Luster was a young widow of attractive person, and a sub-chief directing the marauding band that captured us saw and was conquered by Mrs. Luster's beauty at the time of the attack on our home and instantly resolved to take her along as the favorite of the miscellaneous collection of squaws attached to his camp. As would be the case with any refined woman, Mrs. Luster looked with abhorrence and loathing upon this enforced union with a Comanche warrior without warrant 'or ceremony other than the savage decree, and the cruel circumstances that made her the helpless victim of an unspeakable violation, humiliation, and involuntary debasement. The other Indian braves concurred complacently, and as is their tribal custom scrupulously respected the exclusive rights and ownership of the chief, to his latest appropriation of a fair pale-faced mate. This Lothario of the forest and plain, failing in his avenging designs upon my life as atoning for the escape of his white princess, who on the fleetest horse of all the camp had sped away as if on the shadowy wings of the night, was in no temper to accept resignedly his distressing loss. The sun had now risen, and summoning one of the most, alert and daring horsemen of the tribe as his assistant, two of the swiftest horses were mounted and the trail taken up in determined pursuit of the fleeing prize. For some distance the fresh tracks pointed the way but at length it was found she had doubled back, crossed, and re-crossed on a trail, finally disappearing in the quicksand bed of a wide shallow stream. Bewildered and exhausted the pursuit was abandoned and the dispirited chief rejoined his band, conscious that the ardently coveted quarry was forever lost to him. Mrs. Luster was a daring

INDIAN WARRIORS

Tom Blackstar (sitting), son of great warrior.   Charley Mumcyki (standing),
descended from fierce chiefs.

horsewoman and equally at home whether in the track-
less forests or the unknown prairies.

The third day following her escape she halted that her
horse might rest and graze and being insufferably fatigued
she fell into a deep sleep. Thus off her guard she was
discovered and captured by three Kiowa Indians who
took her to their main camp many miles distant, and
again she was made the consort of an Indian and this
time a Kiowa chief. Mrs. Luster was thus made to
suffer an excruciating penalty for her captivating personal
charm and beauty. She was about twenty-two years old
and a shapely vivacious brunette at the very climax of a
vigorous young womanhood, and in her captivity had
she willed it she could have become the idol of the warrior
chiefs and the reigning queen of either the Comanche or
Kiowa tribes. If she had read the frightful horoscope in
which was foreordained the death of her brother and her
husband in the Civil War and her captivity and mal-
treatment that followed, she doubtless would have pre-
ferred the forfeit of her life to the terrible ordeal. However, the fates decreed, with invincible will she yielded not.

Within thirty days after her adoption into the Kiowa
tribe, during which period she kept tensest vigil day and
night, she found and embraced the means of her effectual
and final escape from savage captors, and return to the
welcoming ranks of civilization something like eight
hundred miles in an opposite direction from that in which
her unwilling, perilous, and distressful journey began.
The Kiowas would turn loose all their horses at night to
graze, except one to be ridden the next morning in rounding up the herd. For one long weary month Mrs. Luster
kept a keen vigil for an opportune moment to slip away,
and at length one dark stormy night it came. As the
Indians slept Mrs. Luster between midnight and dawn
mounted the horse kept at the camp and once more
essayed the daring dash for liberty; a dash, though im-

posing almost unbearable hardship and suffering, this time to be crowned with triumphant success. The deluge of rain in which she sped over the pathless wild obliterated the tracks of her fleeing horse, making fruitless all efforts at pursuit and her escape secure.

The next day, as she drifted along without definite course or aim other than a determined flight from her bondsmen and the chance upon an unknown fate and destination, she mistook some United States soldiers for Indians in pursuit, and in a desperate effort to get away she undertook to outride them. The soldiers mistook her for an Indian and gave lively chase, catching up with and capturing her at the end of a twenty-mile record run under whip and spur. There was much mutual surprise and gratification when identities were established, and the rejoicings on both sides were unconfined. Though they were strangers, Mrs. Luster soon related her harrowing story. It evoked the deepest sympathy from the soldiers, who were lavish in the kindnesses and courtesies extended her. The soldiers afforded her a safe escort to Council Grove, Kansas, at that time one of the nearest outposts of civilization, and here she took up her temporary abode. Being young and attractive, she was soon married to a Mr. Van Noy, and subsequently the couple established a permanent home in Galena, Kansas, where she died in the month of April, 1904. It is not in all the annals of romance or realism where a woman was made the victim of more miserable circumstances. While one shudders at the chapter of horror, a lively satisfaction is experienced in the knowledge that she regained her equanimity and spent the last and longest span of her eventful life not in the mood of brooding bitter memories, but in the atmosphere and spirit of serene repose, reciprocal happiness, and affection. The cruel inhuman massacre of my mother and the inexpressible abuses and sorrows of Mrs. Luster are impressive illustrations of the sacrifices and perils of the pioneer women of the Texas frontiers. That they faced and met these dangers and the attendant direful consequences with unflinching and unwavering fortitude are sufficient themes for every eulogy or tribute that could be perpetuated in imperishable marble or expressed in the best eloquence of speech or pen of all grateful and patriotic men and women now and for ever more.

The morning after the flight of Mrs. Luster and my narrow escape from the infliction of death the Indians broke camp, and after dividing themselves into several groups they proceeded upon their march in different directions. One group took my little sister, whom I did not see again till we met at Fort Arbuckle, Indian Territory (since included in the state of Oklahoma), some two years later. There were eight Indians in the group to which I was attached and it took us ten days to reach the headquarters camp or Indian village on the Arkansas river. On this last leg of our long journey we had to walk most of the way, as the horses were so nearly exhausted they had not the strength to carry us. At the headquarters were the squaws and the children living in tepees scattered along the river a distance of two miles or more. The return of the braves from a long raid was made the occasion of much demonstration, and having a white boy captive produced a sensation in the village. The Indians boys would crowd around and point towards me saying, "Tibow trousop tibow", and this I soon learned signified white person. As is well known the squaws did all the manual labor and camp work generally, such as setting up or taking down and moving the tepees, carrying the wood and water, doing the cooking and all things else. Taking advantage of my helplessness and ignorance, they made me help them in these unmanly menial tasks the greater part of the first winter. At length the boys and the young men informed me that I was being imposed upon by the squaws and that I could do as they did and let the squaws do everything in accordance with a time honored practice and custom. I therefore asserted my rights and forthwith disavowed these domestic tasks and consumed my time with play and helping care for the

CHIEF HORSE BACK

A daring, unconquerable Comanche Chief, who waged relentless war and conducted more murderous raids and directed more horrible massacres than perhaps any other leader of the savages.

horses. From four to eight families would group their
horses together. At that time the Comanches had collected from frequent raids large herds of horses covering
every variety from gentle work stock to untamed wild
bronchos. I joined the Indian boys in catching, riding,
and breaking wild horses, which was an exciting sport and
an excellent pastime.

On horseback we chased deer, antelope, and buffalo
and made frequent kills with bows and arrows, as the
Indians then had but few guns. In the main our food was
buffalo meat, but sometimes in the late winter when
buffalo became poor we would kill and eat the fattest
horse. At this time the Comanches were divided into
four different bands and were headed and directed by
four different chiefs. The Noconas had a chief by name
of Horseback, and his brother Pernerney, one of the most
daring, fierce, and desperate Indians that ever lived,
claimed me as his own. He had an old cap and ball six-
shooter, and one day he loaded it and after painting
himself and bedecking his hideous person with an unusual
array of horns and feathers he had me follow him into the
sand hills. He had with him his shield and lance.
Mounted on his fiery horse he had me take the six-shooter
and told me when he charged me I was expected to take
accurate aim and shoot at his body and when he turned
his back on the retreat I was expected to shoot at his
back. According to this programme, with lance in hand
he charged me and retreated from me four times. I shot
at him as I was directed to do. As he advanced he held
his shield in front, and as he turned for the retreat he
would swiftly shift the shield over on his back. I shot at
him six times and hit the shield each time. He compli-
mented my accuracy and declared I would make a trust-
worthy warrior. The shield was made from the thick
skin of an old buffalo bull's neck, and was fashioned into
a circular cupping shape something like a saucer. It was

Indian in Full Regalia.

covered with heavy buckskin and in dimensions about
two feet in diameter. These shields were practically
impenetrable. Skilfully handled by the Indians as they
were from long practice and usage they afforded great
protection, and many an Indian life was thus saved in
the unequal combat between the Indians armed with
bows and arrows and the white man with rifles and
revolvers.

I was with this band or sub-division of the Comanches
about sixteen months. During the time fifteen warriors
took me and headed in a southeasterly direction. I
thought surely they were bound for Texas on one of their
periodic raids, and I was elated at the thought of getting
back and finding an opportunity to detach myself from
my savage captors. I was especially possessed with this
conviction inasmuch as our mounts were carefully chosen
and our supply of arrows unusually heavy. We had been
out six days when we reached the Washita river, and
surprised seven Caddo Indians on a buffalo chase. These
Caddoes were on horseback and as there was tribal hostility between the Comanches and Caddoes the moment
they saw us they fled at utmost speed. Pernerney, our
chief, gave command, "Kill all of them; they are Caddoes."
We proceeded to execute the command and soon killed
the entire squad of seven. One of the number having an
extra good mount we had to chase ten or twelve miles
before we caught up with him. There were only three of
our party at the end of the pursuit, consisting of Pernerney,
his brother Tutchis-pooder, and myself. Pernerney, being
in the lead, was the first to overtake him and had shot
him twice, from the effects of which he had fallen from
his horse and was sitting up as we all approached. Pernerney handed me his old cap-and ball pistol and commanded me to shoot him in the head, and this I did.
Tuchis-pooder then scalped him, and we took his horse
and saddle and left him lying where he was killed. Out

of these seven Indians slain, six were scalped. The seventh, being a woman, was not scalped, according to tribal custom.

As we retraced our way to where we had started the attack on the Caddoes, we found the other twelve of our marauding band, and in four or five days we arrived at the Indian village we had left for the raid. The scalps of the Caddoes were exhibited as trophies, and a big war dance followed. Much preparation was always made for these "gala fetes," known to the Indians as "war dances." Large arbors were constructed with such materials as poles and brush, the dimensions usually being eighty to one hundred feet square. The entrance to these brush temples was by means of a deep trench or tunnel in the earth. The Indian warriors would place the latest scalps on poles set in the ground and then dance around them, making medicine as they termed it in English, or in their own language "pohockit mahamey." In these exercises they would be in full feathers and war paint with much of their fighting paraphernalia. They would circle in a half crouching attitude, keeping time to the beating of a rudely fashioned drum, emitting unearthly yelps that could be likened unto the composite noise of the bark of the coyote and wail of the panther; in fact a distinctively ferocious, vibrant, inhuman sound calculated to give one the "cold shivers." Nothing could be more strangely weird than these awesome orgies of the Indian war dance, a mingled exultation over their latest deeds of horror and supplication to the "Great Father" to give them more courage and power in their raids and battles that they might kill and exterminate all their foes and enemies. They believed in a supreme being, and instead of saying God as we do they would say "Our sure enough Father," which in their language is "To-bicke." Their faith was that they would all go to heaven unless their scalps were taken, when they would be doomed or forever lost. It was due to this belief that they scalped their dead foes, with exception of the negro who, according to their theory had no soul. However, they would kill negroes so as to get them out of the way and also to prevent them from killing any of the Indian tribe.

During all the period of my captivity my father strove diligently to get some trace of me, to ascertain if my life had been spared, and if so to rescue or recover me. In his effort to learn something of and locate me, my father spent much time at Fort Arbuckle, a post for United States soldiers. These soldiers had an Indian interpreter by the name of Harris P. Jones, who aided my father in the work of inducing the Indians to give me up. The Indians would say that I was dead, but this father did not believe as he had received a letter from an Indian trader in Kansas who had seen and talked with me and whom I had given my father's address with request to write him the particulars of my location and the specific band of Indians. that had me.

As previously mentioned the Comanches were governed by four chiefs, and Chief Horseback headed the band to which I was attached. Chief Esserhaby governed another band, and in many respects was a most remarkable Indian. He had splendid stature and a commanding presence and, for an Indian, unusual intelligence, and inasmuch as I owed so much to him for my safe return and the further fact that he rendered such conspicuous service in leading the Indians from the warpath to the reservations and in establishing friendliness between the Indians and the whites, I shall digress for the purpose of briefly depicting this distinguished Comanche chief. The chieftancy with the Indians was not an hereditary authority but rather bestowed by the elective choice of the respective tribes. Some of the more essential qualifications were physical fitness, wisdom in tribal affairs, a record for dash and daring, and valor and firmness whether in camp or battle.   These were the requisites of leadership by which the braves were guided in choosing their chiefs. Upon this standard Esserhaby was pre-eminently a great and powerful chief, and was so regarded by both the Indians and the whites.   Esserhaby was a native of Texas, and at the time of his birth the Comanche tribe had great

CHIEF ESSERHABEY (Taken from an old picture)

numerical strength and dominated a large division of Texas. They were notably fierce and aggressive, and also artful and courageous in battle, and stubbornly contested every inch as they were beaten back. So long and persistently did they continue to struggle that the remnant of this once vastly numerous and powerful tribe at the termination had an aspect the next thing to annihilation.

Esserhaby was such a dreaded warrior chief that in 1864 J. W. Throckmorton, then governor of Texas, looking to the pacification of the Indian and ending the struggle involving such a frightful loss of life and burden upon the resources of the state, devised a means of communication with Esserhaby and arranged a specific date for a conference or council at Austin, the state capital, the participants to be a large Indian delegation composed of chiefs and prominent tribesmen headed by Esserhaby, and on behalf of Texas the governor and eminent civil officials and commanders of the state constabulary, including several captains of the Ranger forces, who had done heroic and sanguinary fighting upon the frontiers. The deputation of Indians under the leadership of their chief Esserhaby was met at the frontier by Texas Rangers under whose guidance as the guests of Texas they were safely conducted to Austin, where the conference was had on schedule time. This council was historical and in many respects notable. The immensity of the population and power of the United States and the increased population and strength of Texas were made clear by explanation, illustration, and ample object lessons. Chief Esserhaby and his retinue of colleagues were visibly and profoundly impressed with what they had seen, heard, and been taught. They were entertained and maintained at the expense of the state and were captivated by the consideration and kindness extended by Governor Throckmorton and all the other officials and by the people as a

whole. A treaty was entered into by which Esserhaby
and his immediate followers would become the white
man's friends and would discontinue forever all acts of
hostility and depredations, and live on terms of mutual
peace and respect for life and property rights with all
white settlers upon the borderland of Texas. They
further covenanted to exercise their influence to the
utmost in restraining other divisions of the Comanche
tribe and the Indians of all the other tribes hostile to the
whites. With the consummation of these treaties and
covenants and after much reciprocal felicitation and the
bestowal of abundant food and valuable gifts, these
distinguished Indian guests were escorted on the long
return journey to their distant nomadic homes in the
primordial wilds of forest and plain.

Be it said to the credit of this splendid chief and truly
great and "noble red man" that not in the slightest degree
even in the nature of a trespass was there ever any in-
fraction of the treaty terms, spirit, or covenants upon his
part or that of his band or immediate subjects. It can
also be said of him that his constant exhortation to his
fellow tribesmen, whether around the camp fires, upon the
chase or in the councils of the chiefs, was that of abiding
permanent peace, friendship and honesty. In his irre-
vocable and inflexible stand he had much to combat in
the diabolical perversity and fiery impetuosity of other
chiefs, but all the while there was manifest a gradual
waning and yielding of the opposition. The great good
that resulted from the immovable firmness and unfailing
loyalty of this Indian sage and humanitarian could not be
expressed in mere words. Some day will come that tardy
recognition, when on a granite pedestal a great marble
shaft (wrought from Texas quarries), will tower aloft, and,
surrounded by the monuments to others of the long honor
roll of Texan heroes and patriots, will commemorate and
emblazon the magnanimity and unwonted fidelity, the

loftiness of impulse and character of Chief Esserhaby,
once dreaded as an implacable warrior foe, and withal a
big brained masterful child of nature, whose vibrant soul-
strings when touched by the benevolent and patriotic
demeanor and entreaties of Governor Throckmorton
responded with all the unison and perfection in harmony
of the inspired music of the ancient harp or lyre.

Twenty years later, when the several hundred Comanches and Kiowas, the remnants of these once powerful
and numerous tribes, were established on their reservations
across the Red river from western Texas in the Wichita
mountains and adjacent plains, the little city of Wichita
Falls, Texas, the then terminus of the Fort Worth and
Denver railroad 114 miles west of Fort Worth, elected to
celebrate its third anniversary and in a manner and on a
scale befitting its splendid growth and terminal importance. Being then the first and farthest western
railroad outpost, it was resolved to invest the celebration
with such features as would not only be entertaining and
pleasing but memorable and historical as well. Wichita
Falls was then the extreme western railroad gateway to
the vast and but little known Panhandle of Texas, northeastern New Mexico, No-Man's-Land, and all of the
immense area of southwestern and northwestern Indian
Territory, now embraced within the state of Oklahoma.
This region in scope and breadth almost beyond compre-
hensive grasp, and so recently the habitat of the Comanche,
Kiowa and Apache Indians and the un-numbered buffalo,
was now in that first transitional stage that made it
possible and safe for exploration and occupation by the
world's biggest cattle ranches that so quickly followed.
Therefore, the hardy, venturesome denizens of the great
western wilds and those of the older settlements of the
state and other states were invited to attend this celebration of one week, and they attended by the thousands.
The climax of the celebration was the presence of some

JOHN PASAWAKY, Son of Chief Esserhabey.

five hundred Comanche and Kiowa Indians, including several hundred ex-warriors under the command of the grand old Chief Esserhaby, and that of the renowned ex-governor, James W. Throckmorton, and John Ireland, the then governor of Texas. The lusty young city of Wichita Falls was lavishly decorated, and enthusiasm and hospitality in an unparalleled degree abounded on every hand, as there was with one and all a consciousness that this unique and extensive if not prodigious fore-gathering was to be the prelude to a momentous new era, in fact the christening and baptismal ceremony of one of the world's latest and greatest empires; and utterly impossible would it have been for the anticipations and purposes of this multitude to have found expression under a more impressive, auspicious, and inspiring general setting. Every incident and circumstance seemed to conspire to foreshadow and foretell the uninterrupted industrial progress and substantial achievements ordained to follow.

In pursuance of a studiously planned and prearranged program the celebration was fittingly inaugurated with a parade reaching such proportions as to be nothing less than a splendid pageant. Colorful and impressive this parade was headed by Governor Jno. Ireland and the venerable ex-governor J. W. Throckmorton, and other distinguished visitors, including men conspicuous as daring pioneers and for services rendered the state. Next in line were officers and soldiers from Fort Sill army post across the border in Indian Territory, then a company of Texas Rangers and veteran scouts and peace officers of the frontier wilds. Following closely was the Indian contingent, composed of about two hundred erstwhile warriors with chief Esserhaby and other chiefs at their head, all mounted and in full war paints and the same equipment and paraphernalia that had seen service in many raids and battles with the whites; then uniformed fraternal organizations and representatives of civic and benevolent societies with citizens from the ranks of business, labor, and the professions bringing up the rear, making in all a procession exceeding a mile in length. Military and other brass bands were interspersed, enlivening the stately march to the barbecue grounds, where in characteristic western style and hospitality a bounteous feast was served. The repast was greatly enjoyed and especially by the Indians, for whom a superabundance of fat beef had been barbecued. Fervid patriotic and prophetic speeches were the features of the afternoon's program for the whites, and racing and competitive shooting with bows and arrows engaged and entertained the Indians. The entertainment committee enclosed several acres of smooth plateau on an eminence overlooking Wichita Falls with a high board wall and here the Indians bivouacked and thrilled the citizens and visiting throngs with their weird war dances each night of the several days celebration. The Indians lent these war dances all the coloring, zest and uncanniness of such performances during the darkest hours of the bitterly murderous hostilities that had preceded a few short years only. In attendance upon the war dance of the first night there were thousands of eager spectators, and at the height of the performance there was a temporary suspension that there might be enacted a scene that for dramatic aspect and historical effect could have had but few parallels in the more striking and inspiring episodes of this or any other age.

Upon a raised stand or platform stood ex-governor Throckmorton, imposing and majestic in stature and erectness, and with his snow white hair and beard and his undimmed eyes flashing fiery enthusiasm he looked every inch the grandest of patriarchs. By his side the leonine imperturbable Chief Esserhaby, with soldierly mien sat upon a gorgeously caparisoned cream-colored charger. As these two immortals, each a hero philosopher

and law-giver, looked into each other's eyes with prolonged clasped hands, there were vociferous cheers frcm
the excited multitude whose echoes will roll on when
memories are no more.   Let the imagination be exerted
and taxed in an attempt to reproduce this extraordinary
picture with its wealth of coloring, changeful scenes, and
kaleidoscopic background; for the expression of speech
or pen cannot.   In the glow and shadows of bonfires
blazing here and there throughout the grounds, saturnine
subdued Indian warriors, blanketed, painted, and highly
bedecked with feathers, beads, and multi-colored orna-
mentation, silently and noiselessly stalked as only an
Indian can.   Joyous and expectant men and women of
city and country from over Texas and several other
states touched elbows with dignataries of state, soldiers
and officers, civil and military, with a spirit ard sentiment of reciprocal good-will manifest in every act, greeting
or expression.   With the unclasping of hands with Chief
Esserhaby, Governor Throckmorton was formally pre-
sented to the multitude, over whom fell an instant hush
as in resounding voice he related, retold, and explained
the treaty made years before with Chief Esserhaby, and
how this great Indian had kept the faith and proven an in-
valuable ally and instrumentality in holding the hostile
Indians in check, and the final establishment of peace.
In his peroration this venerable and beloved statesman
and patriot paid a beautiful, glowing, and well-earned
tribute to Chief Esserhaby, a colossus of his tribe and race.

During the delivery of the oration by Governor Throckmorton, Chief Esserhaby was near by, mounted on the
beautiful cream-colored horse he had ridden that day in
the parade.   At the conclusion of Governor Throckmorton's address Esserhaby was introduced to the big
concourse assembled, and from his horse he delivered a
response notable for its candor and philosophy and for
flashes of natural eloquence as pleasing and thrilling as

Chief Esserhabey's Grandson, Squaws and Papoose.

they were rare and unexpected. Chief Esserhaby spoke some English and had a very good understanding of it, but he lacked the necessary fluency in English for so important an oration. He therefore delivered the remarkable address in the Indian language followed by a skilful, trained, and experienced interpreter from the government Indian agency. In his introductory remarks Esserhaby told of the inherent convictions of the great Indian tribes that in the invasion and loss of their country and hunting grounds they had suffered a great injustice at the hands of the whites; how the whites were always advancing and taking more and more territory and that eventually the Indians would lose the heritage of their forefathers, the God-given birth-rights of their ancient race. From this he passed into a recital of the perfidy and broken faith on both sides and the consequent decrees of their councils to go on the war-path and in that manner seek reprisals and circumvent the extension of white settlements and colonies and drive back and destroy those farthest out on the frontiers. He then described in dramatic voice and gesture many of the battles he had waged, told of the victims and the scalps taken, and depicted the horrors and agonies of the dying. Within the hearing of his voice were not a few whites who had also participated in the very conflicts and battles he was portraying. Here he related how messages had reached him, as one of the powerful chiefs of the Comanches, from Governor Throckmorton, the big white chief of Texas, asking if at Austin, the capital of the state, a conference could not be held looking to the formulation of such treaties and covenants that would end the strife and put a stop to pillage and massacre; and how he had harkened to the overture and had had the ruling chiefs assemble, and in council consent to the program of Governor Throckmorton.

At this juncture the unlettered natural Indian orator became more fervid, and in ringing accents described what he saw and did at Austin under the directions and guardianship of the great Governor Throckmorton. He narrated the circumstance of his returning to his tribesmen and saying to them that if they persisted in war they were doomed to extermination, that when an Indian warrior fell or perished in battle his place could not be filled, and that to slay one white one there were thousands upon thousands to fill the ranks. Using almost his exact language and expressions, he said the white man was like unto the leaves of their boundless forests or the blades of grass that blanketed the uncharted plains and plateaus of all the distant wilds the Indians had ever seen or known, and that the Indian had no alternative but death or peace. He then explained to them the pledges he had made the great white father, and the tribesmen owing allegiance to him endorsed his pledges and treaties and were thereafter as steadfast in peace as they had been aggressive and merciless in war. In a vein of much feeling and pathos, in which he referred to the sunset of his days and pronounced a burning eulogium upon Governor Throckmorton and others of his distinguished white friends and colleagues, this splendid masterful old warrior chief concluded what was perhaps one of the most remarkable, impassioned, forceful, and dramatic set speeches or orations ever delivered by an Indian in any age present or past.

Resuming the narrative leading up to the preliminaries incident to my ultimate recovery from captivity and restoration to my father, I should explain I had been held by the band of Comanches headed by chief Horseback, and my captivity was known to chief Esserhaby, who now being a friend of the whites was anxious and ready to do all he could toward my release. He pleaded my cause with chief Horseback and spoke feelingly of the

treaty with Governor Throckmorton, whom he termed
"Buck-skin Coat," and represented as a steadfast friend
of all the Indians. Shortly after this Esserhaby visited
Fort Arbuckle and made known to H. P. Jones, Indian
interpreter, and my father, where and by whom I was
held and an understanding was had that Esserhaby
should journey to the headquarters of chief Horseback as
special envoy in behalf of my recovery. According to
appointment he arrived at our camp or village headquarters and was accompanied by two of his squaws or
spouses. They were guests at the camp some five weeks
and during the time there were frequent big councils, the
object of them being the consideration of returning me
to my people. After a display of much obstinacy it was
finally agreed that I would be permitted to exercise my
own choice or pleasure between remaining a tribesman
or warrior and rejoining my father and civilization. Chief
Horseback and many of his band were confident that
after I had habituated myself so unreservedly to Indian
life, and with such apparent reconciliation and satisfaction, I would elect to stay with them. However, in
this they were in great error, as my decision was instant
and unalterable to return as quickly as possible to my
father and kindred. It was therefore decreed that I
should accompany Chief Esserhaby, with a solemn pact
and understanding upon part of all that if Esserhaby
failed to deliver me to my father I would return at once to
chief Horseback's band. Hasty preparations were made
for our departure.

During my residence with the Indians many mutual
attachments had been formed. I was at an impressionable
age, and reciprocated the fondness and affection for me
that had found lodgment with a large number of these
Indians, including braves, squaws, and their boys who
were my closest companions. Therefore, my going
seemed to cast a gloom over the entire camp and there

were enacted many pathetic scenes that I shall never forget. Not a few cried and wept bitterly, and notably one squaw and her son who had claimed me as son and brother and as such were my guardians and protectors, and to whose immediate family and household I had been attached. This squaw was a sister to chief Horseback and she had two brothers besides the one that captured

MISS MARGIE BABB—Baby Siser of Dot Babb

me, Perney and Tutchispooder. The close companion-
ship had cemented bonds of affection almost as sacred as
family ties. Their kindnesses to me had been lavish and
unvarying, and my friendship and attachment in return
were deep and sincere, and I could scarcely restrain my
emotions when time came for the final good-bye. Esserhaby in getting me detached and into his possession had
not only to intercede, plead and confer for weeks, but to
ransom me as well, giving chief Horseback for his use and
distribution several fine horses and numerous saddles,
bridles, blankets, and other valuable gifts.

The ransom now having been delivered to chief Horseback, and all formalities of the farewell and separation
being over, I was duly transferred to the custody of chief
Esserhaby, who, with me, his squaws, and a few warriors,
departed in the direction of Fort Arbuckle, which journey
we made in easy stages. We would meet other bands of
Indians and halt for several days at a place, and were
six weeks reaching Fort Arbuckle. Esserhaby enjoyed
the sport of horse-racing and was capable of shrewd
scheming in winning horses from other bands of Indians.
Esserhaby had with him some very swift horses, and when
we met a band of Cheyenne Indians he matched a number
of races, the winner in each race to take the competitor's
horse. I was a trained jockey and did all the riding for
Esserhaby, and out of six races we won six horses, having
won every race. Before the races took place, Esserhaby
had me to round up six of the best and fleetest horses, and
with him and the horses steal off to a secluded flat several
miles distant and there test or try out the speed of each
horse. A given distance was designated for me to cover,
and as I would do so Esserhaby would count; and when
the six horses had been run over this course at their
utmost speed he had their record. In the final races with
the Cheyennes he entered his proven animals, and as
previously stated won every race pulled off. This success

so pleased Esserhaby that he wanted to postpone indefinitely our return to Fort Arbuckle, or at all events till we could win a large herd of horses from the Cheyennes and others. To this I would not consent, as I was eager to unite with my father, who was reported as waiting at Fort Arbuckle with the hope and belief that I would be brought in. Esserhaby assented and agreed that he would forego the further racing program and hasten on our journey.

We were now on the Canadian river, and in three days reached the Washita and followed the course of this stream till reaching a point where Anadarko now stands. The Washita was running bank full from heavy rains on its head waters, and, as we were on the north side, Esserhaby said that we would have to swim over and proceed down the south side of this river. Everyone in the party, squaws included, was an expert swimmer, and with pack mules, horses, camp equipment, and general impedimenta we plunged into the raging river and without mishap or great difficulty we landed on the south bank at about noon. We camped for the rest of the day, and in the brilliant sunshine of the afternoon dried our apparel, bedding, and general camp outfit. Early the next morning we resumed the journey, and about eleven o'clock we sighted a bevy of white men camped at no great distance. Esserhaby and his lieutenant made for the camp, and upon arriving beckoned or signaled to me and the squaws to follow with the horses and accoutrements.

As we approached, I saw my father, H. P. Jones, the United States interpreter, and two other white men. Arriving at their camp my father kept his back turned to me, thinking he would surprise me, asking me numerous questions, among which when I had seen my father last; and I answered, "I am looking at him now." He could endure the suspense no longer and racked with emotion and crying he ran to me and embraced me with such exclamations as "This is my long lost darling boy." A convulsive joy or hysteria seized and for a while claimed both of us, and the emotions that surged and possessed us beggar and defy adequate expression. It was not only a case of lost being found, but one as if the dead had actually risen. A restoration unbelievable and one that had given an illusory hope, such as the mirage that always remains just ahead but forever continues unreal and intangible. And all this was changed into a reality, and the son so long lost and so often believed or imagined dead under the most cruel and murderous infliction was again in the embrace of an affectionate father. The reunion with my father while yielding unbounded mutual joy had its bitterness from the awakened memory of that terrible scene of a beloved wife and mother in unspeakable butchery forfeiting her precious life through a futile effort to shelter and defend helpless children dearer to her than life itself.

Some hours of absolute rest necessarily followed this meeting that had so taxed the emotions and strength of both, and we did not proceed on our return journey till in the afternoon when we had had time for composure, refreshment and recuperation. My father and Mr. Jones, the Indian interpreter, had become impatient as a result of the prolonged absence of chief Esserhaby, who had been out several weeks on the special mission of my recovery; and when we met them they were on an expedition either to find Esserhaby or provide some other means for getting in touch with me and having me turned over to them. In the middle of the afternoon we broke camp and took up our march to Pauls Valley on the Washita river. This point we reached the next afternoon, and spent the night and several days as the guests of a Mr. Chanler, who had married a Mexican girl that he had rescued from the Indians a few years before. They then had one child, but on coming in contact with them many

years later I found they had reared a large progeny of
boys and girls.   From Mr. Chanler's place we pushed on
to Fort Arbuckle, and there my father had final settlement with chief Esserhaby in the way of cash and horses
which pleased him highly.   It will be recalled Esserhaby
had ransomed me from chief Horseback with several
horses, and for his work and success in restoring me to
my father Esserhaby was liberally rewarded with both
money and horses.   All this was done solely and inde-

H. C. BABB, Brother of Dot Babb.

pendently by my father, who was not assisted to the extent of one cent by the United States government, charged with the security and protection of the lives and property of its citizens and subjects.

As was mentioned some time previously, my sister had been recovered from another band of Indians and had been with father at Fort Arbuckle awaiting my return. In their projected search for tidings of Esserhaby and me, father and Mr. Jones took my sister with them till reaching the hospitable home of Mr. Chanler, where she was made to sojourn pending our return journey to Fort Arbuckle; and here I saw my little sister for the first time after the marauding Indians that captured us were sub-divided, she being taken by one band or division, and I by the other. To realize upon our meeting that her life had been spared and that she was in robust health was a delight and pleasure I am unable to describe. But again I was to drink from the cup of sorrow and bitterness more deeply than ever in witnessing the anguish and consuming grief of my sister, who had just learned that our heroic mother did not survive the deadly thrusts of the blood-stained lance, knife, and arrow. I had to draw on my every resource, courage, and strength to sustain myself through this chapter of horrors, of which every page was crimson with tragedy or replete with fantastic and harrowing adventure and experience. Finally when I realized the curtain was about to descend and shut out the hideous life of savagery, my feelings and spirits began to rise, and with many expressions of gratitude to chief Esserhaby and Mr. Jones, father and I entered upon the last lap that would take us out of the dominions of the Indian Territory and away from its struggles, weirdness, and savage hate and exploit and back to Texas where we would undertake to re-establish the family altar and out-live and master the bitter memories, calamities and adversities of the past.

The following day we once more reined up at Mr. Chanler's house, and being joined by my sister and all mounted on ponies, we hurried on with quickened steps and in four or five days arrived at Red river, the boundary between Texas and the then notorious and fateful Indian Territory. We found Red river several hundred yards wide and almost bank full from prolonged heavy rains, and our only alternative was to swim across to the Texas side. This performance, with the river a raging torrent, involved much peril, daring, and skill. To find a landing place on the farther side and to test the force of the current my father disrobed and swam the river, selected a place the horses could get a footing and ascend the river bank, and swam back to pilot sister and me across. We at once entered the river on our three mounts and

JAMES W. BABB
Dot Babb's grandfather. Born in Indiana in 1787.
Died in Wisconsin in 1873.

reached the farther shore, and in so doing had a severe
struggle in which I narrowly escaped death. Father led
sister's horse, and drawing on his experience and cool
daring their difficulties were less and more easliy overcome
than mine. I was riding a small black bald-face two-year-
old, and when we reached the main channel, very swift
and heavy with swirling sand, the pony stopped swimming
and turning somewhat on his side rather floated with the
current. I being an expert swimmer could no doubt have
swum ashore, but it was important that I should save
my horse. Tightening my grip on him I floated with
him, and finally succeeded in steering him ashore about
two miles below the starting point. Father and sister
landed several hundred yards down stream also, and on
getting out and not seeing me father took to the river
again and swam and drifted down the stream till he saw
me resting safely on the Texas shore. Two white men on
the Texas side quite a distance off saw our difficulties in
the river and hastened to the river to render us what
assistance they could; but they were too late, and in any
case they perhaps could have helped but little if any, as
in such an angry current to save oneself was enough
undertaking for any man. Father thanked them and
explained to them how mother had been slain and his
children abducted by the Indians, and that he had just
recovered his children and was hurrying them back to
shelter and civilization.

We were without food, baggage, or camp equipment,
and in our hungry drenched condition the next move was
a hurried one to Gainesville, Texas, a few miles distant,
and then a small frontier hamlet. We soon arrived at
Gainesville, and in the interim the ride in the wind and
sun had dried out our raiment. Father very quickly
procured an abundance of food. We partook ravenously,
and felt much relieved and more than ever thankful that
we had preserved our lives in the latest heroic struggle

swimming Red river. The people of Gainesville, on
learning who we were and our experience and adventures,
plied us with myriads of questions, which we answered
as best we could. We were offered every conceivable
courtesy and hospitality, but our chief aim was to hurry
on, and with the least possible delay reach our kindred
and the scene of our former home and habitation. Father
hastily provided the necessary food, clothing and blankets
for our further journey, and we were off for Wise county,
the last leg of many hundreds of miles of travel that in
point of thrilling circumstances, weird and harrowing
scenes, and experiences of suffering and sorrow that
could have but few parallels in the most vividly colored
stories wrought from the imagination, aside from a painful
realism, so burned into the soul and memory that only
time could assuage but never wholly or partially efface.

Our first night out from Gainesville we camped on
Elm creek, and starting early in the morning and pushing
hard all day we arrived by nightfall at the home of a Mr.
Boothe, twelve miles north of Decatur. There we found
my brother, H. C. Babb, and my baby sister, who had
been spared by the Indians. We were now about two
miles from where we were captured by the Indians. Our
arrival was unexpected, but the rejoicing on both sides
beggars description. In this way the fragments of our
once joyous and devoted family were reunited. The first
emotions of uncontrollable gladness and rejoicing in
clasping each other in arms of affection soon gave way to
the realization that our beloved mother was not there,
and that with her the only reunion vouchsafed was when
each and all of us should answer the last summons. With
this as our only solace we resolved to so live and die as
to be worthy of the memory and love of that dauntless
mother, who bravely and unflinchingly sacrificed her life
in extending sheltering arms around her trusting helpless
little ones. For a short while we lived with the Boothe

family and were then placed in the home of a Mr. John
Thompson just south of old Bridgeport, where we remained a few weeks till our father got possession of a log
house built by Mr. Couch on our land near the old place
where we were captured by the Indians.

In this log house we undertook to establish another
home. The care of the house and children was largely
entrusted to me. My father had exhausted his resources
in his efforts to recover my sister and me, as the pursuit
was a long and expensive one aside from the money and
horses turned over to the Indians as our ransom. Therefore my father had to accept gainful work where he could
find it for our maintenance, and we lived largely alone.
The Indians were still dangerous, and at regular intervals
continued their depredations upon the frontier settlers.
To suppress such and protect the Texas frontier the
United States government began the erection of a fort at
Buffalo Springs, Clay county, Texas. My father was
engaged on this work, and to this place we removed with
the family of Mr. John White. The war department

My father moved to Wise Co. in 1859. I was then 10 years
old.

Mr. J. S. Babb was one of our neighbors, and we lived as
neighbors until after the Civil War.

And after the war the Indians were troublesome on the frontier
and in the fall of —— they went to the home of Mr. J. S. Babb
and murdered Mrs. Babb and left Margie, infant, in the house,
and took Dot, Bankuella, and a widow lady by the name of
Roberts with them and kept them for several months. At the
time of the killing of Mrs. Babb, Mr. Babb and his son, H. C.,
were on their road to Arkansas with a bunch of cattle and horses
for sale.

When Mr. Babb returned to this Co. he found his wife killed,
his home destroyed and his children carried off by the savages.

He left H. C. at my father's home and started to Ft. Sill, where
he found his children living with the Indians.

He succeeded in getting his children away from the Indians
and brought them back to Wise Co., where they lived several
years.

Dot soon became a man and married Miss Pattie Graham, and
moved West, and is now living at Amarillo.

                                        RUFUS BOOTH.

RUFUS BOOTH

decided that the army post should be further out and
abandoned the project at Buffalo Springs. Instead they
established Fort Richardson at Jacksboro, Texas, and we
moved thither. Father continued in the service of the
government for some months and I and the children kept
house for him. We had a few cattle scattered over the
range and looked after by my brother, who worked for the
Earharts. In the spring of 1868 father arranged with
George Stephens, who lived near Decatur, to take my
sisters into his home, and that released me to engage in
work for myself.

I began work with my brother and Baus Baker, and
shortly thereafter we commenced gathering cattle for a
drive to Kansas markets. As the cattle were gathered
they were driven to and held herded on Hog Eye prairie
in Jack county. Here we accumulated many cattle and
moved them to a range below Decatur, and held them
there until completion of the herd. Assisted by Jim Hall
the cattle were kept together and guarded by alternate
watches day and night. We now had assembled ready for
the trail some thirty-five hundred cattle, consisting of
cows, calves, yearlings, and steers from two to twelve
years old. This was a miscellaneous assortment of long-
horn cattle. Some of the older steers had such long and
wide spreading antlers that they were frightful to behold,
and in this day of short-horn cattle they would be a
drawing card in a museum. The herd belonged to five
different owners, Jip Earhart, Wit Adair, Jim Hardin,
Baus Baker and Joe Henry Martin. With the five owners
and Lansing Hunt, Jim Hall, Booze Earhart, Bud and
Jim Ham, Jim and Ben Fowler, and Cook Brazelton, we
started on the trail to Kansas early in the summer. We
crossed Red river northwest of Gainesville, and as usual
at that season Red river was up and we were all day
swimming the cattle over. Our wagon loaded with
supplies and baggage was drawn by oxen, as was usual

in those days, and after getting the herd safely over the river the next big task was to get the wagon and oxen across. We procured some dead cottonwood logs and tied them under the wagon hub on each side so that the whole outfit would float like cork. We hitched the oxen to the end of the wagon tongue with a long chain. Two of us took positions on opposite sides of the oxen so as to point them across the river, and others got into the wagon to weight it down, and in this fashion the craft and the crew consisting of oxen and men were launched for the crossing. The oxen swam bravely and kept the course pointed by the two pilots, the logs and wagon floated serenely, and everything pointed to success, until we

GEO. STEPHENS, Decatur, Texas

reached the opposite bank of the river where we had to
untie the logs to disembark the wagon.   In this operation
there was some blundering work, and the wagon sank to
the bottom in deep water.   The water was so deep and
swift that we had to wait until the next day for some
abatement of the river that we might unload and then
rescue the wagon, which we did and soon proceeded to
take up the trail again.   We traveled what was known as
the Shawnee trail, and had but little more trouble till we
reached Arkansas river.   Before it was possible to reach
Kansas we had frost, and had to go into winter quarters
on Rock creek.   There being only a settler every here and
there, we had plenty of open country and hired settlers
to winter the cattle on prairie hay.

In the meantime Joe Henry Martin had moved to
Kansas on the White Water near Augusta, and the Adairs
and Earharts had moved to Eureka, Kansas.   As soon as
the cattle were delivered to the settlers to winter I started
across the country from Eureka to Augusta.   There were
not a dozen families along the entire route I traveled.   I
was in rain and snow the entire day's journey.   I did not
get through to Augusta the first day.   I followed the
course of the streams on which the straggling settlers
resided.   The homes consisted of dugouts, hay houses,
log cabins and other such make-shifts.   As night approached I applied at each house for lodging and notwithstanding the sleet and snow I was turned away by
first one and then the other, each one saying I would be
welcome at the next cabin.   In this way I kept going till
darkness was closing in, and here I found another cabin.
I made known my desire to stay over night, and received
the same old answer that they did not have room but
that I would find a house across the creek kept by two
men who would be delighted to have me.   I explained
my predicament and how I had been treated.   Being near
desperation I said, "I'll go no further, but right here I'll

put up for the night." Again my prospective host objected, saying this time that he had no horse feed. I pointed to a big hay stack near by, and, saying my horse could eat hay, I dismounted. My grim determination overcame him, and he took my horse to feed him and directed me to go into the cabin. This I did, and thenceforward was never treated more cordially by anyone than by this man and his good wife. I found my right foot partially frozen, and accordingly the wife kept back the biscuit from the stove oven that I might use that space and heat to thaw out my foot and remove the boot, a most painful operation. With homely remedies I saved my foot and was able to walk the next day, and also to get the boot on by leaving off the sock. The next morning I resumed my journey to Augusta, which consisted of one store building conducted by Dr. Stewart. The upper story of this building was used for the neighborhood school. Joe Henry Martin lived about one mile west of Augusta, and with him I established myself for the winter.

With the coming of spring and grass I went to Eureka, got a yoke of oxen, and drove them to Lawrence, Kansas, where the herd had been collected from the various sections in which the cattle had been wintered. There were now fifteen hundred head of Texas steers from four to twelve years old that we had driven from Texas the year before. These steers belonged to Baus Baker and were driven on through Kansas to Lee Summit, Missouri, by Reece Barton and me after we had herded them until they had fattened on the grass. In driving through Kansas we had much stubborn opposition. The Kansas settlers were afraid of Texas fever in cattle, but it was understood that Texas cattle wintered in Kansas were safe and were permissible. Our greatest difficulty was in convincing the Kansans we had wintered the herd in Kansas. Now and then they would meet us ten and twenty strong with shot guns, bull dogs, and other devices

of destruction, but being from Texas with the terror of
Texas cowboys we bluffed them with our old cap-and-ball
six-shooters and moved right along to our destination
without a scratch. We shipped about half the herd from
Lee Summit to St. Louis, and here we fell in with a man
by name of Charley Dunlap, a Mexican reared in Texas,
who had four hundred Texas steers. We consolidated the
remainder of our steers with Dunlap's, and drove over-
land to Kansas City and from there shipped to St. Louis
via the North Missouri railroad. I went to St. Louis with
Mr. Baker, the owner of our cattle. In Kansas City we
put up at the State Line hotel, where we remained three
or four days while getting the cattle shipped. We held
our cattle in the valley between the mouth of Turkey
creek and Kansas City along the Kaw river. Wyandotte
was located on the hill just across the Kaw river from
Kansas City. At that time there was neither live stock
exchange, nor stock yards, there being merely shipping
pens. As before stated we shipped the cattle over the
North Missouri railroad and crossed the Missouri river on
the bridge. On reaching St. Charles, Missouri, we crossed
back, this time on ferry boats, four cars of cattle at a
time. Our cattle were unloaded in the North Missouri
Stock Yards, and then driven on foot up town to the sale
yards. At that time in St. Louis there were only the
North Missouri and Pacific Stock Yards. I assisted the
boys in driving cattle from both yards up to the city.
There was no bridge over the Mississippi at St. Louis at
that time, but they had just started work on the first
bridge. The cattle were ferried over the river, some loose
in the boats and others in the cars rolled on to the boats.
East St. Louis was then a small village. I remained in
St. Louis about two weeks, and had a fine time assisting
the boys handle cattle. I was supplied with a good horse,
but my saddle was what the cowboys called a human
saddle, which was next thing to being bare-back. I also

An Ex-Warrior and His Family.

had fine sport rowing, canoeing, and swimming in the
Mississippi river, and did not want to leave.

Mr. Baker, my boss, said the time had come for us to
depart, and we did so by way of Kansas City, where we
joined our outfit for the return trip to Texas, the greatest
state the sun ever shone upon. Reunited with our outfit
we started for Texas. All in the party were Texans except
Reece Barton. In the party were Baus Baker, Jim and
Charley Burton, Nigger Cap, myself, and six or eight
others. We crossed Kansas and what was then known as
Indian Nation. We came by Parsons, Kansas, at which
point there was then only one merchandise store. The
return journey was most delightful and at times exciting,
as game big and small abounded in indescribable plenty
on every hand and everywhere, to say nothing of fish in
every stream. We traveled in a leisurely fashion, and
employed our time shooting and feasting on the choicest
game of all the land. This, coupled with the wild solitudes
of the vast untenanted region we traversed, made the trip
one never to be forgotten. At length we reached Red
river, the Texas boundary, and crossed into Texas at
Colbert's ferry, north of Sherman. After landing in Texas
we started for Decatur, touching at Sherman, Denton,
and Pilot Point. Upon arriving at Decatur I took my
two sisters and established a home for them and me. My
father, having lost everything at the hands of the Indians,
did work on the outside wherever available for the needful
support of my sisters, and could therefore be at home
with them but little. In this way we lived for about two
years, when father decided to take my sisters to relatives
in Wisconsin.

Thus I was once more given my liberty to set out and
do for myself. My brother, H. C. Babb, was working
with cattle on the range for Dan Waggoner. I joined my
brother in this work in 1870. In 1871 Joe Loving made
a deal with Mr. Waggoner to take charge and handle the

cattle for a period of five years on the shares. I was engaged by Mr. Loving, and continued with the outfit. We had considerable trouble with the Indians, who would break in now and then and steal our horses. In the fall of 1871 Joe Loving took me and two more hands and joining Frank Mull of Parker county with four hands, whose names were John and Henry Strickland, Dave and Mat Loftin, together with pack horses and four extra saddle horses each, we started for a round-up of Jack and Palo Pinto counties. We gathered all the big early calves we could find that were not marked or branded. We took in the mothers of some of the calves and some we did not. When we did not want the mother cows we cut them back, and if they returned we shot them in the nose or

Comanche Medicine Man and Tepee.

punched them. In this manner we gathered about five hundred "mavericks," and drove them to the ranch in Wise county, where we marked and branded them, putting on the marks and brands of Mr. Waggoner and Mr. Mull. Having finished this job Joe Loving took an outfit and went in below Decatur and brought back all of the big calves he could see or get regardless of who owned them. Very soon the citizens discovered their calves were gone and learned who had gotten them, and so angry were they that there was talk of mobbing Mr. Waggoner, who knew nothing whatever of this stealing of cattle. Mr. Waggoner immediately bought out the interest of Joe Loving and made just and satisfactory settlement with the rightful owners of the stolen cattle. By way of digression I should say that in the early days of the cattle industry unbranded cattle belonged to the outfits who could get to them first and then have the means in the way of enough fighting men to hold and keep them. After such a fashion many of the great herds and fortunes in cattle were started and reinforced from time to time.

In 1872 Mr. Waggoner decided to move his cattle to the far west and this he did by driving to Clay and Wichita counties and locating there. I went with the second herd, and we arrived at Big Wichita river just below the present city of Wichita Falls, October 10th, 1872. I remained with the cattle the winter that followed and was assisted by my brother H. C. Babb, and cousin Tom Babb, Sam Merrick, and Jim Barrenton, half-breed Cherokee Indian. During the winter the cattle gave us but little trouble, as grass and water were everywhere plentiful. There was not then a wire fence between Red river and the Gulf of Mexico. Will and Lish Ikard came in with a small bunch of cattle just below us that winter. Jim Curtis also brought some cattle the same winter, which he located in the forks of Wichita and Red rivers not far from us. In the spring of 1873 Waggoner brought up another herd

and about the first of April we commenced to gather a
herd to be driven to Kansas. When they were gathered
on the south side of Wichita river and in readiness for the
start, it began raining and rained hard for two days. We
waited for the rain to subside, but on April 9th the rain
turned into a heavy snow which continued till the fall of
snow reached ten inches. We therefore turned the herd
loose and when we overtook them the next day we had
to travel thirty miles. This will indicate how swiftly
cattle drift with a snow storm. We were four days getting
the cattle back and ready for another start. We lost some
ten horses frozen to death in the snow, and in recovering
our cattle we came in contact with about twenty men
who had run up from the south to see if we had stolen any
of their cattle. They had their trouble for nothing as we
had no cattle but our own.

We were again ready to start for Kansas on April
14th, and that night the Indians stole all the horses we
did not have tied up. On the morning of the 15th very
early old Nigger Samy Kirby and I were out to ride
around the cattle when we met four or five hundred steers
running from towards Red river. These steers belonged
to Will and Lish Ikard who had also started to Kansas,
when the Indians the night before had raided them, taking
all their loose horses and a few that were together out on
the grass with saddles on them. So being unhorsed and
in a bad plight both outfits had to halt and go to Wise
and Parker counties for a recruit in horses before it was
possible to start the herds. We were only 45 miles from
Fort Sill, Indian Territory, where the United States
government had a large army post for supposed protection of keeping the Indians under control, and this will
denote how well they succeeded. We soon saw we would
have to provide our own protection and look sharply out
for our scalps, or lose them, as others had done. About
this time the Indians on a raid killed and scalped a man

by name of Alison, on Pond creek between the present cities of Wichita Falls and Iowa Park in Wichita county. On the same raid they chased Ed Terret, who outran them and escaped to Missouri, where he would have to be shown in the future. These men were working for Glen Halsell at time of the raid.

In the summer of 1873 Pat Kemp, Harry Green, Tom Flannery and I had charge of and guarded the cattle just north of the Wichita river. Many days we had to swim the river, which we enjoyed very much. Every day was brimful of excitement of one kind or another. If nothing else pressed, we chased and shot down buffalo, antelope, deer, and turkey. The prairies and plateaus were literally swarming with the big game, while the valleys and wooded margins of the streams were swarming with turkeys, chickens, and quail. The turkeys were so plentiful as to afford us an abundance of fresh eggs whenever we wanted them to eat. No such abundance of game had been found in any known locality, and we killed not only for food but pastime. In the fall Pat Kemp left us and went to south Texas, and in the winter Bill Graham took his place. Harry Green went to work for the Ikards and Jimmie Roberts took his place, and in the winter of 1873 Jimmie Roberts, Tom Flannery, Bill Graham, and I looked after the cattle and kept them together.

Aside from other thrilling experiences there was now and then a tragedy interspersed which added zest and variety to the arduous as well as hazardous lives we lived in those times of stress and peril. I recall one tragedy in particular as having features partaking of both the pathetic and comic. In April 1873, Mr. Dan Waggoner came up to the ranch from Decatur to look over the cattle and conditions generally. He traveled in a buggy accompanied by Col. Booth and a very small man whose name I have forgotten. Mr. Waggoner as usual had his old shot gun with him. While Mr. Waggoner, Booth and

JIMMIE ROBERTS

Born in Mississippi, January 3d, 1852. Came to Texas 1870, and entered employ of Dan Waggoner 1871, and continued with him for many years, rising eventually to ranch manager and foreman. During this period Mr. Roberts and Mr. Babb were closely associated and fast friends. Jimmie Roberts was noted for his bravery and daring as a buffalo hunter and Indian fighter, and was also a terror to cattle thieves and other bad men with whom he had many encounters, and all of which he survived. As he is to-day a prosperous citizen of both Texas and Western Canada, having property and business interests in both, Jimmie Roberts is a notable example of the type of fearless, cool, dependable men who at length reclaimed and civilized the Wild West.

their companion were away from camp looking over the cattle, Joe Scamkaskey, the Dutch cook, and Jack Scott engaged in an angry quarrel over a saddle. Jack applied an unmentionable epithet to Joe, who ran at Jack for a fight. Jack then drew two cap-and-ball six-shooters and cocking them in Joe's face, said, "You Dutch wolf, my name is Jack, who is always ready." Joe backed away from the six-shooters and retreated to the camp fire, as it was a bitterly cold day. Thinking the difficulty had ended, Jack, Pat Kemp, and I went into the tent where we slept. We were talking along when Joe jumped into the tent with Waggoner's shotgun and said, "Take back your abuse of me, Shack." As Jack started to draw his six-shooters, Joe let drive with one barrel of the shotgun at Jack, and the charge tore off Jack's coat sleeve and then into the ground, taking with it one of my boot heels. At this Joe sprang out of the tent, threw down the gun, and ran for a saddled horse standing near. Jack was hotly pursuing Joe, having shot at him twice when Joe abandoned the horse and fled into the brush with Jack after him. Jack shot at Joe five or six times in the chase, missing every time. Eventually the Dutchman distanced Jack and got back to the shotgun, picking it up just as Jack approached. With shotgun in hand, Joe said, "Stop, Shack, I don't want to kill you." Jack, instead of stopping, leveled his pistol, which failed to fire. As he did so Joe pulled the shotgun trigger, and twelve buckshot pierced Jack under the right arm, from which he sank upon the ground, holding a cocked revolver in each hand. I said, "Jack, are you hurt?" and his dying answer was, "The Dutch hyena has killed me." This took place about ten o'clock in the morning. In the afternoon we rolled Jack's remains into a blanket, and buried them in a slough four or five miles below where Wichita Falls now stands.

My cousin, T. C. Babb, and I found Jack Scott in the winter of 1872 near where the city of Henrietta now is.

He wore Indian moccasins and good clothes, being without gun or pistol and afoot. We took him to our camp where he remained until he was killed. He helped around the camp and seemed a man who had been well reared. He had varied accomplishments, among which was that of the buck dancer. My cousin was a fiddler, and many dreary hours in this isolated camp life in the wilderness were passed with the dancing of Jack to the music of my cousin's fiddle. Jack was about thirty years old, and said he was from Kansas. He may have had a mother and father, brothers and sisters, who looked for his return in vain, and who never knew of his fate, and his last lonely resting place in nature's wildest solitude.

During these times we had frequent encounters and narrow escapes from the Indians, and so evident was the peril that it was difficult to keep a sufficient number of men on the ranch. However, Jimmie Roberts, Tom Flannery, Nigger Cap, Lem Fowler, and I remained on the job; and at times when others would not, regardless of pay or pleading.

As a digression, and also as illustrative of the wildness and remoteness of this extreme frontier of civilization, and the protecting arm of an organized government, I shall relate an incident in which a fellow employee named Pat Kemp figured with me. In the spring of 1873 Pat and I were not closely occupied, and decided we would travel about, learning more of our unknown surroundings. One day our explorations carried us up Red river, and at the mouth of China creek we were taking in a large scope of country with our field glasses when we discovered a company of United States soldiers in camp at Fort Augur across Red river, on the Indian Territory side. Acting on the impulse we proceeded to cross the river and pay them a visit. As soon as the soldiers saw us approaching from the distance, the bugle was sounded and some eighty cavalrymen put out in our direction, meeting us in about one mile from the fort, whither they escorted us. We had our noon-day meal with the soldiers, and early in the afternoon we remarked the time had come for us to return to our ranch duties on the Texas side. The captain inquired, "Whose ranch, and how far distant?" We explained the ranch belonged to Dan Waggoner and was located on the Big Wichita river, some twenty-five miles away. The captain said that there could be no such ranch or he would have known of it, and directed us to remain and go under guard the following day to Fort Sill. I inquired why we should be detained and sent to Fort Sill, and his answer was that we could then give an account of ourselves and establish whether or not we were Indian spies. I replied that we were not Indian spies, though we saw Indians most every day and did our best to keep away from and out of sight of them. I further emphasized that we were nothing more or less than ranch hands, and urged that we be released to return to the cattle under our care and protection. The captain ordered us to remain till next morning, which of course we had to do, and when the morning had come the captain announced his decision to send us to Fort Sill. I said, "Captain, we will obey your orders, but we wish you to send us by the ranch headquarters, so we can explain our abscence from the ranch, otherwise there would be apprehension that we had been slain by the Indians, and no little search made for us by rescuing parties, composed of our co-workers on the ranch." The captain said bluntly, "There is no ranch, and consequently no one to notify, and I'll therefore send you directly to Fort Sill." I protested, and disavowed our being liars, and at this juncture Pat Kemp said, "Captain, you are a d——d liar, if you say there is no ranch over there, as we have stated," and the captain stated that a "little stay in the guard house will do you good, young fellow."

Chief Quanah Parker and three of his six wives, the one in the center being a daughter of the notorious Chief Horseback.

I undertook to smooth matters, and proposed that we be sent to the divide, where our log ranch house could be seen through the field glass, just as we had discovered the fort. The captain agreed to this, but warned us beforehand that if the ranch house failed to show up our punishment would be severe. We were impatient, and said, "All right, let's be going, and before starting give back to us our guns." The captain handed us our guns, but kept our ammunition, saying that if we had stated the truth as to the ranch house he would deliver the ammunition as he had released us. Pat says, "Captain, if we meet or see any Indians will you give us our cartridges?" "I guess so,' answered the captain, and Pat said, "If you don't, we will outrun the Indians, as we have done before." The captain being interested, said, "Did you ever outrun the Indians." And Pat declared that had the captain witnessed the race he would surely have decided in our favor. Pat said further, "One time Babb and I were together, and Babb was mounted on a good fast horse, and I on an old slow stud pony, and I said, 'Babb, don't run off and leave me,' and Babb answered, 'I won't,' and he did not either, and by holding our ground we stood off sixty Indians, and did not have to kill them to do it." Under escort of forty soldiers we put out in direction of the ranch, and when we reached the divide about sixteen miles from the ranch, we showed them the old cottonwood log ranch house covered with dirt, in plain view to all, and the officer in charge said he was convinced. Upon his handing us our cartridges, we bade the soldiers farewell, and in a brisk gallop made our way to the ranch headquarters, where we were warmly received by our associates. They were gratified that we were unharmed and back with them for the work, and the added defense against the Indians.

As Fort Augur was one of the earlier outposts during the stirring Indian days, a brief description of it should prove both instructive and interesting. This fort occupied an eminence on the north side of Red river, just below the mouth of Augur creek. The fort was surrounded by entrenchments about six feet each in depth and width, with the dirt thrown up high on the outside for breastworks. From the fort a trench some six feet deep led down the hill to a big running spring, from which the water supply was derived. This trench was to prevent being cut off from water in case of a siege or a long sustained attack by the Indians. Outside of the fort and all around it were holes some five feet deep and four feet square, further protected with poles about four feet high. In these holes soldiers did picket duty for the fort. The soldiers were taking no chances of being surprised and scalped by the Indians, whereas we cowboys rode the ranges either singly or in groups of two or three and frequently slept out of nights, with neither shelter nor protection, and no bedding except the blanket always carried attached to the saddle. Of course all this was attended by great danger, but being a part of the game we could not and did not falter. We were always prepared and ready to fight, as we did do frequently, with hair-breadth escapes. It is astonishing how one can become so accustomed to peril as to go right along, perfectly resigned to any fate or eventuality. The Indians had a far more wholesome fear and dread of a few cowboys than of many regiments of soldiers.

The hardy Celt, Pat Kemp, who for so long a time was my constant companion, was wholly insensible to fear and danger, and our very recklessness and daredevil methods awed and intimidated the Indians and more than once saved our lives. Pat and I were one day further exploring the beauties and wilds of Red river valley when to our utter surprise we beheld a small peach orchard, with trees heavily laden with luscious ripe peaches. This was in July of 1873, and the orchard was situated a few miles north of the present city of Wichita Falls. At first we could scarcely believe our eyes, not being able to realize the possibility of a peach orchard beyond the boundaries of all civilized human habitation. We partook of the peaches and were convinced, and a rarer and greater treat was never enjoyed. We explored a little more and found an abandoned log hut overlooking Red river, which hut no doubt still stands intact. We afterwards learned that a venturesome man by the name of Gilbert undertook to establish a home at this place. After living there two or three years undisturbed he was discovered by the Indians and with his family barely escaped to the white settlements in the vicinity of Gainsville.

In the spring of 1874 Clay county was organized, as the farthest western organized county, and Henrietta was established as the county seat, where a short time before the pioneer Cusier family was broken up by the Indians. Some of the members were massacred, while the others were carried into captivity. At Henrietta a small log house was erected for the sessions of the court, presided over by Judge Lindsay, as the first judge, and with L. C. Barrett, now of Amarillo, as one of the first practising attorneys at the Henrietta bar. It happened that I was one of the first jury to serve, and then also had my first jury service. There was no felony docket the first session, the term of the court being engaged in misdemeanor cases solely. We members of the jury gave verdicts of guilty for all with minimum fines in each case. For jury service in this first session of the court, now more than thirty-eight years ago, I have not drawn my scrip, which, with interest compounded, would to-day make a comfortable sum, if collected.

A great deal has been said and written with reference to the methods employed by the old-time or original cow-men in accumulating and increasing their herds. I am in position to speak with authority on this subject, and would say they were naturally as honest as the average of men. They were creatures of environment and proceeded along customary lines, as men have always done before or since. It was the custom to take dry cows and strays, also mavericks, which were cattle that may have been marked but unbranded. The idea or plan was to take in and properly mark and brand and appropriate such cattle before the real cattle thief could do the same thing. At that time there was no law against stealing cattle, but there was an unwritten law that was severe enough when the thief was actually caught in the very act of stealing the cattle. Especially rigorous was this law when invoked or applied in case of the professional or weaker thief, who paid the penalty dangling at the end of a rope over a limb of a tree, or was doubled up by the ball of a Winchester or revolver. As best I can recall, in August of 1874 was the last Indian raid with fatal results. This raid was through Montague and Wise counties, and being taken unawares, the entire Huff family was killed by the Indians. At that time I was still on the ranch in Wichita county.

In the fall of 1874 I discontinued the work on the ranch, and returned to Wise county. There were then but three families residing between Wichita and Wise counties, a distance of eighty or ninety miles. At first I did not seem to fit in just right in a community of civilized people, but gradually I learned to adapt myself to the prevailing conditions, and being susceptible to the charms of the girls I met I became more than reconciled. To be sure, there were not many girls, as there were not many families, but there were enough to interest and engage me, and above all, one in particular, to whom I addressed unwavering and ever increasing attention. On October 7, 1875, I was married to Miss Pattie Graham, the seventeen

year old daughter of Mrs. M. A. Graham, at old Bridgeport, Wise county, Texas.

My wife's mother was a native Texan, and was
married in Red River county, Texas, before the Mexican
war. Her mother was Mrs. Isabella Gordon, better

Mrs. T. A. (Dot) Babb was born December 31st; 1858, and is
descended from that sturdy pioneer stock from whom Texas and
all other states of this union derived the elements of strength
and greatness. Reference is made in another place in this narrative to Aunt Ibbie Gordon, Mrs. Babb's paternal grandmother,

MRS. T. A. (Dot) BABB

a very notable and illustrious woman of the trying and strenuous early days of Texas. Another conspicuous ancestor is John Hanks, the maternal grandfather of Mrs. Babb. An heirloom very highly treasured by Mrs. Babb is herein reproduced in the form of a Commission of Justice of the Peace of the township of Sevier, Miller County, Arkansas, issued by Governor Crittenden, Territorial Governor of Arkansas, at Little Rock, Oct. 21st, 1824.

Thus it can be seen 88 years ago Mrs. Babb's forebears were serving their country with credit and fortitude on the border line of an ever broadening west. Mrs. Babb at 54 is remarkably well preserved and true to the inherent spirit of heredity is ever on the alert for the best channels for the exercise and direction of her energies, looking to the betterment of mankind and a higher and stabler civilization generally.

known as Aunt Ibbie Gordon, and came to Texas with her father in 1823, being then eighteen years of age. So distinguished was Aunt Ibbie Gordon, my wife's maternal grandmother, in the early annals of Texas, that I deem it entirely appropriate to reproduce a part of the biographical sketch appearing in a book now extant, entitled "Prominent Women of Texas," written by Mrs. Elizabeth Brooks, as follows: The Hopkins family came to Texas from Kentucky when that was made a free state, they being slave holders. Hopkins county, Texas, was named for L. and Dick Hopkins, uncles of my mother.. They settled on a small creek in what is now Bowie county, the extreme northeastern portion of the state, and in the following year the daughter married John Hanks, and the couple moved to Jonesboro, then an important trading post on the southern bank of Red river, and on the main line of travel on the western frontier. There the husband died three years later, leaving one daughter as the issue of the marriage, this daughter being the mother of my wife, Mrs. Babb, and the young widow went back to her father's house. Two years afterwards she married Captain Jim Clark, a native of Tennessee, with whom she returned to the former domicile in Jonesboro, where they continued to abide pending the preparation of a new home further west. It was while living there that the war for Texas independence began to be waged, and it was there on the highway of travel that recruits from the northeast tarried in their passage to the scenes of conflict. Their zeal added fuel to Mrs. Clark's patriotism, and her patriotism gave aid to their cause. It was there that in 1832 one of the illustrious men of Texas history first set foot on Texas soil. This was Sam Houston, American by birth and instinct, once a congressman and governor of Tennessee, and already famous as warrior, statesman and politician. He was commissioned by Andrew Jackson to negotiate trades with the Indian tribes of the southwest, and was on his way to hold conferences with their chiefs. To reach the scene of his conference he followed the trail that led to the Indian Territory, and came to the northern bank of the Red river, opposite which stood the trading post of Jonesboro. He there fell in with Ben Milam, the future

MRS. GRAHAM, Mother of Mrs. Dot Babb

hero of Goliad and San Antonio, of whom he inquired the probabilities of finding something to eat. Milam told him that he himself was the guest of the family living on the other bank, and that accommodations could no doubt be had there. They accordingly crossed the river together, and, entering the only house on the southern bank, were welcomed by Milam's hostess, Aunt Ibbie Gordon of our narrative. In relating the sequel of this meeting, she says that with her own hands she cooked the first food that Sam Houston ever ate in Texas, and that her house was the first in Texas to shelter the future president of the great republic. Our distinguished guest tarried but a day, and resumed his southward trail to Nacogdoches, in those days the Mecca of all western enterprise. His visit, though brief, was long enough to make an impression on his admiring hostess, who described him as handsome, courteous, intelligent, and most fascinating in manner and conversation. Two years after this episode Mrs. Clark removed with her husband to their new home, in what is now Red River county, and on the site where is situated the present flourishing town of Clarksville. They then laid its foundation, and began to erect that which culminated in its present importance. It was in 1835, the year following their removal, that Mrs. Clark met another of the heroes that are famous in Texas history. This was David Crockett, who gave up his life in the bloody siege of the Alamo. He was following the usual trail on his way to the headquarters of the Texan army. She heard of his approach and resolved on giving him the welcome she had extended to the many patriots who had passed that way before him, but having removed to Clarksville, somewhat off the main line of travel, she knew she could not see him unless she intercepted him in the course of his route. This she determined to do, and after a horseback ride of a few miles brought up at the home of a settler, where she found the object of her eager pursuit.

A few words served to introduce those earnest advocates of a common cause, and a mutual hatred of oppression soon gave to each a knowledge of the glowing patriotism that burned in the bosom of the other. After a few hours of mutual solace and encouragement they parted, he for the field of his exploits, and she for the home where dwelt the brightest spirit of Texas independence. This home was saddened not many months afterwards by the fate that befell the brave Crockett, and only three years later it was made desolate by the death of Captain Clark. In the year following this second bereavement Mrs. Clark was married to Dr. George Gordon, who died in

GRANDMA IBBIE GORDON, Grandmother of Mrs. Dot Babb

1872, after a happy married life of thirty-three years, during which he and his wife lived in her old Clarksville domicile. ·There in the house she entered sixty years before, Aunt Ibbie Gordon lived to reach the patriarchal age of ninety, not seared but only mellowed by time, bright in mind, cheerful in spirits, and, prior to her last illness in 1895, sound in body and rejoicing in the reverence and affection of all who lived around her. Her life had moreover been blessed by several sons, whose honorable lives reflected the virtues of their venerable mother, and brought to her declining years the peace that only a mother's heart can feel."

My wife's mother, Mrs. Graham, died some five years ago at the home of her sons, W. H. and G. G. Graham, in Artesia, New Mexico. Mrs. Babb and I lived in Wise county on Dry Creek until the summer of 1879, when we moved to Wichita Falls, Texas. On our arrival there we found only three families making their home at that point. These families were those of Judge Barwise, Judge Sealy, and Mort Wattenburger. In the fall of 1879 Mr. J. H. Harris settled with his family in Wichita Falls. At that time the total number of families living in Wichita county perhaps did not exceed fifteen. Our union was blessed with six children, three of whom being born in Wise county and three in Wichita Falls. We had the misfortune to lose four children, all of them being buried at Wichita Falls. Only two of our children survived, Tom and Annie, both of whom are now grown, married, and making substantial headway in life. I engaged to D. Waggoner & Son for work on their ranches, and could only be at home sometimes once a week and other times once a month, as my duties kept me out on the ranges, looking after the cattle, and far removed from home. This worked an especial hardship on my wife, who had to live alone during my prolonged absence.

By this time there were ranches established here and

MAXINE BABB, Granddaughter of Dot Babb.

there all over the country, and dividing lines between the
different ranches were agreed upon and respected by
mutual understanding. It was necessary that cowboys
travel these dividing lines daily to keep the cattle thrown
back to their respective zones and prevent, as far as possible, the indiscriminate mixing up thereof. However,
despite all such precautions the cattle would cross these
lines at night, and especially in winter when they would
drift before driving storms. With the coming of spring,
the cattle by the thousands would be found many miles
from the ranches on which they belonged. It therefore
required many men and big work to get the cattle back
to their allotted ranges. It must be borne in mind that
in those days there were no barb-wire fences, and it was
owing to this fact that each big ranch had to have a small
army of cowboys looking after their employer's interest.
It was the custon, and a necessary one in those days, to
have, during the spring and early summer, what was
known as the annual "round-up." and on the occasion of
these round-ups it was not unusul to see twenty-five to
thirty chuck wagons, with from thirty to sixty men to the
wagon. Seeing these large forces concentrated preparatory to entering upon the several months of round-up
work reminded one of the vanguard of an invading army,
and this impression was largely accentuated by the supply
of arms and ammunition carried by the cowboy fraternity
in those days and times. The arms consisted of such
miscellaneous armament as large revolvers and Winchester rifles of all styles and calibres. The revolvers
were worn strapped around the waist and the Winchesters
were carried in holsters pendant from the saddles. In
this way they were always prepared for battle, and whenever there was combat there was fatal results to one or
both of the combatants. The round-up work would go
from one ranch to another until the whole country had
been worked over thoroughly, after which all would meet

Quanah Parkers Stage Coach.

at the starting point. Before entering upon the work the first step would be to elect a general round-up boss, who had supreme command of all divisions and sub-divisions of the army of cowboys engaged in rounding up the cattle from the ranges far and near. After all the cattle had been brought together each ranch owner, or ranch boss, had charge of his given bunch until the cattle were all concentrated in one general herd. The general boss would then take charge and let each outfit take its turn cutting out the cattle belonging to it as designated by marks and brands. The cattle would then be held night and day in the separate herds until the ownership had been established, even to the last hoof. I have been engaged on these general round-ups for six weeks to two months at a time, and have gathered cattle from the Colorado river to the North Canadian, north and south, and from Childress county, Texas, half way across the Chickasaw Nation east and west.

We continued our residence in Wichita Falls from 1879 until 1898, with the exception of one year spent on Nine-Mile creek, ten miles from Fort Sill (now in the State of Oklahoma). The Indians with whom I lived during captivity at length identified me at Wichita Falls, and from that time they urged me to remove to the Indian Territory. They contended that I was by captivity and adoption a Comanche Indian, and had as much right in the Territory as the rest of the tribe. At this time Captain Lee Hall of Texas was Indian agent at Anadarko, Indian Territory. Acting on the suggestion of my Indian friends, I went over to Anadarko and called on Captain Hall and said to him that he should issue me a permit to make my home with them. Captain Hall inquired into the history of my case, and found that the Indians claimed tribal kinship with me and were not only willing but extremely desirous of having me settle with my family in their midst. After explaining to Captain Hall my captivity

QUANAH PARKER, Chief of the Comanches.

Quanah Parker, a once powerful Comanche chief, and the son of the white woman, Cynthia Parker, who was captured when a girl by the Indians and taken as a wife of the distinguished Chief Peta Nocona, and subsequently recovered by General Sul Ross at the end of a battle in which General Ross slew Chief Nocona and most of his followers.

Cache, Okla., Feb. 10, 1910.

This is to certify that I know Nadinewmipe or Dot Babb. He was captured by the Comanche Indians a long time ago when he was a boy about 13 or 14 years old. He was with the Indians about two years,

QUANAH PARKER,
Chief of the Comanche Tribe.

and residence with them as a boy and ther adoption of
me into their tribe, Captain Hall gave his consent; whereupon I moved my family from Wichita Falls, Texas, to
the Indian country, and everything moved along smoothly
until Captain Hall's removal as Indian agent. Following
Captain Hall's retirement from his position as Indian
agent, a special agent by the name of White was sent to
investigate my right to settle and live with the Indians.
Upon his submitting his report to the Indian agent, which
report was unfavorable to me, a squad of Indian police
were sent to me with orders to move out of the Indian
Territory; but the Indian police advised me to disregard
the order and remain, advising me that in doing so I
would have their support and protection. The great old
Indian chief, Quanah Parker, Esetye, Wild Horse, and
several other sub-chiefs importuned me to remain, saying
they would not suffer me and my family to be put out.
I had about decided to continue my residence with the
Indians; but my wife pointed out that we might be
annoyed and that, at all events, we should return to
civilization, where we would have necessary school ad-
vantages for our children. With her persuasion along this
line I consented, and we abandoned a good home we had
erected and returned to Texas.

We returned to our home in Wichita county, Texas,
and lived there from 1879 until 1898, when we moved to
Clarendon, Donley county. We resided in Clarendon
until 1906, when we moved to Amarillo, Potter county,
Texas, where we now reside. Knowing the Panhandle as
I do, I am firmly convinced that Amarillo is the future
metropolis of the great Panhandle country, and destined
to become one of the large cities of Texas.

A great deal has been written from time to time as to
the inner life, domestic traits, habits and temperament of
the Indians, concerning which there has been no little
exaggeration. My residence and intimate relations with

the Comanche Indians, during which time I observed
very closely, peculiarly qualify me to speak correctly and
truthfully on such subjects. In their relations with one
another they were considerate and tolerant, and did not
fall out, fight, and kill each other as do the white men.
The only real fighting I ever saw among them was con-
fined to the squaws. Occasionally a squaw would do

Amarillo Residence of Mr. and Mrs. Dot Babb—The group at front of house consists of Mr. and Mrs. Dot Babb and daughter, adopted son, Robt. Babb, Dude Babb (the dog, 10 years old) and Rawhide (the horse)

something to excite the anger of the others, when they would combine and give the offending squaw a terrible beating. Usually this had a very salutary effect, and the victim of the flogging would rarely, if ever, repeat the offense. Neither the Indian men nor squaws would whip or bodily punish their children. It was a recognized tribal custom for the men to have two, and from that to as many wives as they desired. There were no marriage ceremonies, and when a girl reached the age of fourteen to sixteen she was given away by the father and mother, unless, in exceptional cases only, an admirer would steal the girl, somewhat after the custom so prevalent with white men. Generally the men would be loyal to their wives, and their wives to them; but now and then, just as is the case in civilized communities, a man would find an "affinity" in another man's squaw and take her away from him. The penalty in such cases was the recognized right of the man losing the squaw to take all the horses and property of the Indian stealing the wife, until the victim felt that he had been fully satisfied. Under no circumstances did they resort to fighting and killing over the loss of a squaw, which was always adjusted on a strict monetary or property basis. Another striking trait was that of the interest the several squaws belonging to one man took in each other's children, and in fact such children were as affectionately cared for as if the offspring of that particular squaw. In the main the squaws lived together in harmony. After reaching a certain age, the men would abandon the old squaws, and supply their places with younger women; and in this way the older and discarded squaws had the right and liberty to become any other man's wife that would elect to accept or adopt her, and the new alliance could be formed without the consent of the former husband.

All the Indian subjects showed great respect and obedience to their chiefs and head men. During the

Quanah Parker's Home.

summer the different chiefs would assemble the tribal
members in their jurisdictions, and separate camps would
be constructed and maintained accordingly. Such camps
were usually pitched on the bank of some running stream
for the convenience of both grass and water. It was also
a custom to move these camps every eight or ten days,
so as always to have plenty of grass near-by for their
numerous horses. The Indians were gregarious and would
live in towns, with their tepees arranged with the same
precision as the streets of a city. They would set the
tepees with the doors facing to the east. If it were cloudy
when they put them up, resulting in some deviation from
the right direction, this fact they would discover as soon
as it cleared up. With the sun as a compass, they would
then rearrange all the tepees. The day before they would
break up and decamp for a new location, the chief would
get on a horse and ride up and down the streets shouting
at the top of his voice a description of the location to
which all should move the next day. Sometimes they
would cover twenty or thirty miles in one day, and on
the day of break-up for the move everyone got in a great
hurry, and more especially the squaws, who had to gather
up all the belongings and attach them to the pack horses
and mules. They would tie the tepee poles on each side
of a horse or mule by one end and let the other end drag.
These poles were from twelve to twenty feet long, and on
such they would pile their impedimenta, until one could
scarcely see the back of the horse or mule bearing the
burden. The children that were too large to be carried
on their mothers' backs and not large enough to ride
alone were tied on some old horse which moved with the
procession. As an improvised ambulance for the sick or
wounded they would tie a buffalo skin from one pole to
another and fasten one end of the poles to the pack
saddles, the other ends dragging on the ground. While
such locomotion seemed rough, it always answered the

QUANAH PARKER, in Costume.

purpose. It frequently happened in moving that some of
the pack mules or horses would become frightened or
stampeded, and in their flight scatter the sundry packages
and household plunder for miles in every direction, re-
quiring several days to collect up the fragments and re-
assemble the animals and their belongings. In moving
from one district to another the men and boys would
divide their time between chasing deer, antelope, and
buffalo, and driving the horses. They would begin
moving operations just as early in the morning as they
could; and as to who should get started first in the moving
there was great rivalry, since the first to reach the new
camp ground had choice of location.

As before stated, the tepees were arranged in the order
of streets. One of the reasons for this was that of enabling
the warriors to parade first one street and then the other
in their efforts to arouse and incite the Indians when a
raid had been planned and recruits were wanted. Notably
was this the case preparatory to getting together a company of warriors for an incursion into Texas and New
Mexico. The warlike and restless spirit of the Indians
was dominant, and they could not be quiescent for any
long period. When seized with the mania for a raid, the
leading men would make medicine to determine when and
where the raid should take place. After this point had
been settled they would cover their faces with hideous
war paint, and array themselves in their most frightful
bonnets of feathers, spears, bows, and arrows, and in this
shape, led by a man beating a drum, they would parade
all the different streets. As the procession moved along
volunteers would join as the spirit moved them. These
parades in this fashion would continue each day with
increasing frenzy of war whoops and hideousness of paraphernalia for from twenty to thirty days, such performances ending only after the requisite number of warriors
had volunteered and enlisted for the raid in contemplation.

Unlike civilized governments, they had no compulsory military service, and their fighting squads were recruited wholly from volunteers. I have seen and been with them when after a strenuous three weeks recruiting campaign they would be ready to start out with two hundred to three hundred warriors. When an Indian warrior was killed or slain in battle, the other warriors and squaws that were related to the slain made what they thought to be expiation, by inflicting such punishment upon themselves as abstaining from food and drink for a good length of time and cutting themselves severely with knives and doing other severe bodily injury to themselves. The surviving warrior comrades would shave the hair from the right side of their heads, and the squaws of the deceased warrior's family would sometimes cut off all their hair. I have seen the squaws take butcher knives and carve their arms and legs and also their bodies in a most frightful manner, and when the wounds would be partially healed they would reopen them so as to prolong and intensify their bodily suffering. In entering upon these bloody orgies they would take a butcher knife in one hand and a whet rock in the other, and after carving a while would sharpen the blade and carve some more. Occasionally this mutilation was carried to a fatal extent. I had a very exciting experience and also narrow escape during the enactment of one of these performances. I had just been added to the headquarters camp after my captivity on the Arkansas river when certain warriors had returned from a raid in which a number of their comrades had been killed, and the mother of one of the slain was so crazed with grief as to be bereft of her reason. I had been sent with some Indian girls to a running brook near by to bring water to the camp, and I heard horrifying shrieks and moans. On looking around I beheld this Indian squaw approaching with a large butcher knife and a whet rock, and the next thing I knew the infuriated woman made a fierce attack with murderous intent upon me. Being unwilling to offer myself as a voluntary sacrifice, I fled with great celerity, and seeing that she could not overtake me she halted and carved herself to pieces. It matters not how long I shall live, this harrowing picture will remain ever fresh in my memory, and during the intervening years, not infrequently in my dreams has the apparition of this frenzied and demoniacal squaw appeared unto me.

Many years after these troublous times I had occasion to visit Fort Sill, the headquarters of the Indians, and what was then known as the Comanche and Kiowa reservation; and there I renewed my acquaintanceship with many of the old time warriors and with them reviewed the thrilling scenes of the Indian raids and exploits of the years agone. Certain prominent Indians were missed from the ranks, and concerning them I made inquiries with much interest and solicitude. Notable among them were Pernurmey and his brother Tutchispooder. Pernurmey was the leader in the raid in which I was captured, and he claimed me as his son. In captivity he frequently stated to me that he would die before he would let the white people take their country away from them. In answer to my inquiry as to what he considered his country he designated the country from Fort Worth east to Red river and west to the Colorado river, and from this line

---

Waneda Parker, the daughter of Quanah Parker, the late Chief of the Comanche Indians, is a young woman of striking appearance and of much cultivation. Her mother is a full blood Comanche, while her paternal grandmother was the famous Cynthia Ann Parker, a white woman who was taken into captivity in girlhood, latterly to become the consort of the famous Comanche chief, Peta Nocona, slain in a hand to hand combat by that immortal hero, General Sul Ross. One of Waneda Parker's elder sisters was married to a Mr. Emmet Cox, a white man, and from this union there was a daughter who was educated in the best seminaries and is now an accomplished school teacher in the Philippine Islands.

WANEDA PARKER
Daughter of Quanah Parker, late Chief of the Comanche Indians.

north to the Arkansas river.   At Fort Sill I learned that
Pernurmey had made good his resolve to die in defense
of what he considered his country, and was killed in Lost
Valley, Texas.   I was told by the surviving Indians at
Fort Sill that five Indian warriors and one squaw headed
by Pernurmey left the reservation at Fort Sill, saying they
were going to Texas to get some more scalps of the white
men, before laying aside the tomahawk forever.   This
was in 1873, and on the raid Ira Long, of Wise county,
Texas, with a small company of rangers overtook them,
killing four and wounding two.   As the wounded were
never heard of again they must have perished from their
wounds.   The Indians would relate to me their experiences in the various fights and raids that they had made
into Texas for many years preceding.   They referred to
the time when the white men had no guns except the old
muzzle-loading patterns, and in the attacks they made on
the white men they would wait until the white men would
shoot and then dash at them while they were reloading
these guns.   They described these white men as having
very long whiskers and being exceedingly brave and expert
marksmen.   They further said the white men did not
seem to fear the charges made by the Indians and paid
no attention to what was going on until their guns were
reloaded, at which juncture the Indians would have to
get out of the way as quickly as possible, as by experience
they could well anticipate what the results would be.

Too much praise cannot be given the organized forces

Cattle Ranch located near Alanreed, Texas, owned and
operated at present time by Dot Babb, who is surrounded by a
few of his Red Poll cattle, while his favorite horse grazes in the
background.   A never failing creek runs near by with numerous
springs affording abundant stock water, fine fishing, and duck
shooting.   This splendid ranch consists of several sections rich
grazing and agricultural lands.   Stock raising and stock farming
are the leading features of this picturesque and generally most
excellent ranch.

Scene on Cattle Ranch owned by Dot Babb at present time.

of rangers and minute men maintained by the several frontier counties for the effective defense and protection afforded the widely scattered citizens and settlements in the trying Indian days. It can also be said that great credit is due the hardy courageous cowboys that worked in conjunction with the rangers in repelling the Indians from time to time and pursuing and driving them out of the limits of the settlements. These forces did much more to safeguard the lives and property of the citizens of the frontier than all of the United States soldiers combined. The custom of the Indians oftentimes was to divide into small groups or raiding parties, and in this manner they would elude the United States troops, who were better adapted to attacking the Indians in larger bodies. A small band of Indians would engage in a raid, and owing to the red tape enveloping the army posts would cover a large scope and destroy great life and much property and get away before the troops could get into action. As the rangers and cowboys were always well mounted and armed, and could get on the trail and in pursuit of the marauding bands of Indians almost immediately after they entered the boundaries of the settlements, the Indians knew and feared these forces. There could be no better illustration of how the Indians regarded the relative effectiveness of the cowboys and the United States troops than a dialogue that took place between an Indian and the commandant of a certain army post. The Indian accosted the officer and asked him if he would trade him one of the mounted cannon at the post, whereupon the officer answered that he would not, saying, "If I trade a cannon to you, you will use it in killing my soldiers." The answer of the Indian was that such would not be the case, as he wanted the cannon to shoot cowboys with, and would kill the soldiers with clubs.

In the interest of history it can be recorded that the

rangers and cowboys are undeniably entitled to the glory and credit of eventually driving and keeping out the Indians from the Texas frontiers, and not the United States troops. I wish to make especial mention in this connection of George Stephens, an ex-sheriff of Wise county, who was captain of a small company of rangers, as it is a noted fact that he and his men alone killed more Indians and repelled more Indian attacks and afforded more protection to the frontier citizens of the western tier of counties than was ever accomplished by the soldiers. It was the custom of Captain Stephens and his men to attack and pursue the Indians regardless of any disparity in numbers and strength. An instance was the attack made by Captain Stephens on the Indians in Lost Valley, Jack county, Texas. In this attack Captain Stephens had but a very few men with which to engage several hundred Indians that were making a raid through Jack and adjacent counties, during which the Indians massacred not a few people, among whom I recall Bill Glass and a young man by the name of Bailey. A strange coincidence in connection with the killing of the young man was that his father had been slain by the Indians on a similar raid when the younger Bailey was only a child. Notwirhstanding the large number of Indians in this memorable Lost Valley raid, Captain Stephens and his small band of intrepid forces succeeded in routing them and putting them to flight in such a manner as to save the lives of many people and much property. A short time after this particular raid another band of Indians, consisting of several hundred warriors, intent upon murder and plunder, entered Texas. Once more Captain Stephens and his company undertook to drive them out of the settlements, and did so. So hurriedly did he pursue them that he overtook them on the Little Wichita river in Clay county, Texas, some ten miles southwest of the present city of Henrietta, and in this pursuit Stephens had **not** exceeding ten men. When the engagement opened up he discovered that he had encountered three hundred Indians and a band numerically so strong that he could not hope to cope with them. The battle opened and had raged furiously for some time when Captain Stephens, seeing that they could not hold out in their resistance much longer, had his men dismount and seek shelter in the timber and canyons, abandoning their horses altogether. In this way they kept up a desultory fight under cover and during the night effected their escape. They set out for Decatur, Wise county, which was distant about eighty miles, which distance they covered on foot without either rest or food. This was accomplished without the loss of a man and after inflicting severe punishment upon a large body of Indians. I only recall the name of one of the ten men with Captain Stephens on this occasion, and that was John Hogg, a brother of the late distinguished Governor J. S. Hogg of Texas.

A great deal has been said and written about the Mustang horses so numerous in the Northwest, and especially in Texas, from the upper Cross-Timbers, and over the Panhandle of Texas, and in what was then known as "No Man's Land" and is now Beaver county, Oklahoma. As a digression, I would say that in the early days No Man's Land was the place of refuge and rendezvous for many of the most vicious outlaws and fugitives

---

Indiahoma, Okla.,
March 22, 1910.
I will now drop you few lines this morning. I received your letter few days ago. I was very glad to hear from you. Now, my friend, I haven't got them pictures, because I was very busy. But I am going sent them to you soon as I get them fixed. Now if you can get that Biscuits when you get it and sent me just few of them. Well, how are you getting along I hope you are well. How is people at Texas anyhow. We are all getting along very nicely. My friend, I guess it must be all for you this time. I must close it now

I am, your dearest friend,
PARKERHEIMER.

Parkerheimer, Squaw and Son.

that ever inhabited this continent. These outlaws had
No Man's Land practically all to themselves, and it was
a very rare instance that an officer of the law ever succeeded in going into and taking out of this district any of
the aforesaid outlaws. Frequently an officer would go in
and never be heard of again.

Resuming the subject of the Mustang ponies, I would
say that as far back as 1866 to 1867, I traversed all of the
country above described in the two years I was with the
Comanche Indians, and the supposed Mustang horses
consisted of animals that had been abandoned by the
Indians and originally stolen from Texas and New Mexico.
The Indians made a practice of stealing and having
plenty of horses, and when hotly pursued by Texas
rangers, cowboys, and United States soldiers, it would
frequently happen they would have to abandon many of
their horses, as in their hurried flight they could not
drive the horses fast enough and would necessarily leave
them behind. In this way the horses became scattered
all over the country. I recall one instance when the
United States troops captured a band of Indians that had
an unusually large number of horses, and the officers in
charge gave orders to kill most all of the horses in the
possession of the captured Indians. In executing these
orders the troops rounded up and killed on this particular
occasion about two thousand horses.

During my compulsory sojourn with the Comanche
Indians I was not permitted to accompany them on any
of the raids into Texas, but they were glad to have me as
one of their warriors on raids into Mexico, and on such
raids I accompanied them twice, each raiding party
consisting of about seventy-five men. In each exploit
they secured a considerable number of horses, and on the
last raid we killed seven Mexicans and captured two
Mexican girls and one boy. These children ranged in age
from eight to ten years, and were still with the Indians as

Daughter of Chief Tabernanika, now lives near Fort Sill.

captives when my release from them was effected. Space would not permit me to depict and relate the circumstances of the many harrowing Indian massacres of which I had knowledge during the dark days of the Indian depredations, but I will relate one instance, terrible in its cruelty and unusually pathetic in many respects. This particular instance was that of the massacre of the Russell family that took place in the year 1868, some four miles southwest of the location now occupied by Chico, Texas. Mrs. Russell was a widow that with her four children had lived alone for several years. She had three sons, about twenty-one, sixteen, and ten years of age respectively, and her daughter, Martha, was eighteen years of age. In the attack from the Indians all were killed including the mother, except Bean and Martha. Bean was absent at work as an employe of a United States government saw-mill about ten miles from his home, which was the old Joe Henry Martin place. The Indians destroyed this home on Saturday, and on Sunday morning Bean Russell returned to spend the Sabbath with the family, as was

---

Cyril, Okla., Apr. 21, 1910.

Dear Bro. Dot:—I was very glad to get your letter. I want to go up there but I do not know when will Quanah Parker go there, so if you will let me know when he is going I will go with him. I do not know the way to there. I will send you a few pictures that I have here and next time I will send some more. We are all well here, hoping you the same.

Your Bro.,

Name means "lost a sitting down."   Tom Watsacoder.

Cyril, Okla., Nov. 3, 1910.

Dear Brother:—I will write a few lines to you this morning. Well, we are all still in good health, we have been in a good condition since you left here. Quanah has gone and we did not know that they have to pay some money to go hunt there so I did not go. We did not know the way to go down there. I will not write a long one this time, but will do better next time. I hope this letter will find you all well there so must close for time. Answer soon.

From your brother,

Mr. Dot Babb.   Tom Watsacoder.

Tom Watsacoder, who claims Dot Babb as his brother, and other Indians in regalia.

his usual custom.   There he was confronted by the ghastly sight of his murdered mother and brothers, but he could find no trace of Martha.   He at once hastened to the nearest neighbors, three or four miles distant, and reported the horrible massacre.   At this time there was not exceeding ten families in the county.   In this raid there were not less than three hundred Indians.   The mystery of all was what had become of Martha.   With many the conclusion was that the beautiful young girl with golden hair had been made a captive by the Indians who would take her away with them.   However, this theory was shaken on seeing and talking with Uncle Dick Couch and his sons, who resided in the neighborhood, and who had just successfully withstood an attack from the same band of Indians, having in reality not only resisted them but driven them off and given pursuit.   Uncle Dick and his sons contended that in the encounter they saw the entire band, and that Martha was not with them, and that they must have killed her after leaving the Russell home.   Following this there was a general search for Martha, whose body was found by Uncle Dick Couch on his way home on the day we had buried the other three slain members of the Russell family.   He at once reported such to the neighbors, who proceeded to bury her remains with the other members of the family.   It was found that these ruthless Indians had not only killed but had scalped Martha and left her entirely nude, and when found the wolves had badly mutilated her remains.   It was supposed the Indians scalped her that they might take her very fine and luxuriant suit of golden hair.   Neighbors on inspecting the Russell home found that the widowed mother and sons had made a most desperate resistance, each dying with one or more weapons in hand and surrounded by large puddles of their own blood.   They had fought with desperation and no doubt had wounded or killed some of the attacking Indians; but in case of killing

Comanche Dwelling.

the Indians it would not have been known, as it was their
invariable custom to carry off their dead. This frightful
tragedy took place within twenty miles of a United States
army post, Fort Richardson at Jacksboro, Texas, and is
a further evidence of the inefficiency of the United States
government in protecting its citizens. This is only one of
a countless number of similar massacres which will give
some idea of the sufferings, dangers and hardships of the
daring pioneer people who blazed the way that civilization,
security and prosperity might follow in their wake, and
further serves to remind all of the debt of gratitude to
the brave pioneers of Texas that can never be paid.

During my early ranch days with Dan Waggoner in
the counties of Clay and Wichita there were immense
herds of buffalo roaming the prairies in all directions, and
I was accustomed to having some fine sport pursuing and
occasionally killing the buffalo bulls that were wont to
show fight. Pat Kemp, my companion to whom I have
already frequently referred, enjoyed this sport with me.
I recall a very ludicrous experience one day when Pat and
I were chasing some large buffalo bulls. During the chase
I had killed three or four, and in the heat of the pursuit I
had lost sight of Pat. Going in search of him I saw Pat's
riderless horse coming in my direction. I felt very much
alarmed and hastened to look over the surrounding
country, when to my great surprise a few hundred yards
distant I saw Pat astride a buffalo bull. Thinking that
he would need assistance I put spurs to my horse and
hurried to him and on overtaking him inquired why he
was riding the buffalo. Pat's reply was that "Old Buckskin," the horse that he had been riding, "could not overtake the young buffalo," and being desirous of killing
some buffalo yearlings he had mounted the buffalo bull,
believing that in that way he could get to the front, and
that when up with the young buffalo, he could dismount
and kill some of the yearlings that were leading the herd.

But instead the old buffalo had sulked and would not run at a fast pace. I then asked him how he expected to get off the buffalo, and Pat said, "You get my Winchester when I throw it down, and I will show you how to get off," whereupon he threw down the Winchester, and I got off of my horse and secured the gun, so that I could shoot the buffalo, if necessary. At this juncture Pat drew his large bowie-knife, with which he stabbed the buffalo several times, the buffalo soon thereafter falling dead in his tracks. As the buffalo fell Pat jumped, remarking, "That is the way to get off an old buffalo bull." This memorable buffalo ride was on Gilbert's creek in Wichita county, Texas, in 1873.

Pat and I had many experiences with and many narrow escapes from the wild animals with which we came in frequent contact, as Pat and I were always in quest of something new as a means of occupying the more or less idle time that was not required in giving attention to the cattle. On one of these explorations through nearby plain and woodland, in which we were also enjoying the excitement of chasing the wild hogs that roamed in the bend of the Big Wichita river, just above Wichita Falls, near its present cemetery, an old bloodhound that we had with us found and treed four panther cubs. Three of these cubs were in a big cottonwood tree and the other in a hackberry not so large. Pat and I shot the three in the cottonwood and they came tumbling to the ground, two of them being dead and the other badly wounded. When it hit the ground it was crying just like a child, and on hearing its wails the cub in the hackberry tree came tumbling down also, as if it had been shot. Between Pat and old Red, the bloodhound, and myself we managed after a desperate struggle to capture this cub and tied him securely, and as we were finishing, the two old or parent panthers appeared on the scene in response to the screams of the wounded cub. Before we could realize

their presence and threatened attack old Red had engaged them both in unequal combat. Old Red did not
seem to be very much in their way, and I would like to
have adequate expression of how I felt when I saw them
approaching, but I have not the language to do so. One
of their first efforts was to undertake to release the cub
that had been tied, and all the while they were menacing
us with an attack that we knew to be right at hand. I
seized my Winchester rifle and Pat his .45 Colt's pistol,
which he used with one hand, holding on all the while to
the young panther with the other. There was no time
for us to prepare a campaign of defense, and in the emerg-
ency we had to look out each for himself and shoot as
rapidly and unerringly as possible. This we both did,
and to my great relief, as well as astonishment, we succeeded in killing both of the infuriated beasts, just as
they were in the act of seizing and tearing us to pieces.
We could not have escaped as we did at all had it not
been for the brave and unflinching work of old Red, the
hound, who seized the mother panther in the beginning
of the attack and during the fight never released his hold,
notwithstanding the horrible wounds and laceration he
received. In this way the mother panther, the more
vicious of the two, as would naturally be the case, was
badly handicapped. We would shoot and both panthers
would continue to advance, and we must have shot them
ten to fifteen times before killing them. They were intent
upon but one thing, and that was our destruction, and
had we retreated the least bit, or had missed our aim in
any instance. we could not and would not have survived
the combat. We carried our young panther to the ranch,
and with the general treatment we administered it became very docile and was valued highly by us as a rare
pet. Just as we were becoming much attached to it, Dutch
Joe came up from Sherman and we made him a present
of the young panther, which he took with him on his

Indians Butchering a Cow.

return to Sherman. The wild hogs referred to on the Wichita river were the offspring of a stock of hogs owned by the man Gilbert, who had the hardihood to establish his home on the Red river some fifteen miles distant before the Civil War. These hogs had wandered from Red river to the woodlands bordering on Wichita river, and there multiplied in great number, and were just as wild and vicious as any of the other dangerous denizens of the plains or woods. We derived a great deal of excitement from the chase of these wild hogs with our blood-hound, old Red, as the chase was always full of zest and danger.

Another danger more dreadful than wild beasts, and one that in the summer and fall seasons lurked ever near, was that of the fatal fangs of the venomous rattlesnakes that abounded in great numbers on every hand. These were the black and diamond rattlesnakes, frequently attaining a length of six to eight feet, and having from ten to twenty rattles. These deadly monsters of the plain were always in an aggresive mood and were ever ready to contest the right of way with all comers whatsoever. At the approach of man or beast their rattles sounded that awful alarm so often the prelude to their fatal and deadly strike. They would coil instantly, giving out the hideous rattle all the while, and with incalculable rapidity strike their full length, injecting a venom equal in fatality to that of the world-famed cobra. It was not the particular propensity of the rattler to hunt out victims but rather to hold its ground and attack and fight viciously upon the sudden and unexpected approach of almost any living creature. To retreat in the face of an enemy or of threatened danger or combat was no part of the code of a rattlesnake, whose self confidence and bravery were always supreme. The greatest peril from these terrible snakes, so very like the hues of the parched grass concealing them, was realizing by their rattle that they were near you and not knowing in what direction to jump or flee, and realizing also that if you moved precipitately likely as otherwise you would land within the radius of their strike, so deadly as to be almost beyond all hope. One of the safeguards employed was that of heavy boots with high tops, but withal occasionally a very large rattler would plant his fangs entirely above the boot's protection. You have read and heard recited the story

Apache Girls Going for Water.

of the tranquil abode in the prairie-dog hole, of the rattler, the prairie-dog, and the owl. All of which is the veriest fiction, since whenever the rattler entered the hole the dogs and owls either went out of the hole or into the snake, for the snake subsisted largely on both. With the coming of settlements, rattlers disappear rapidly, as no one was ever in too great a hurry not to kill the rattler if he had or was able to secure the means with which to dispatch this most hated and dreaded of all species of venomous and deadly reptiles. To surround the camp tent or the lonely bunk upon the slope with a hair rope was an effectual expedient often employed against an unwelcome nocturnal visit and a stealthy occupancy of either the tent or bunk with such dire results as death, either from fright or poison. The rattler, like the tarantula and other terrible, creeping, crawling things that once menaced the life and comfort of the unprotected sleepers upon the ground, would not cross a hair rope.

Upon occasion I have been in such dangerously close quarters with the rattler that I would cheerfully have exchanged him for the biggest lion or the most ferocious man-eating tiger that ever trod the jungle. I shall only relate one particular harrowing experience with a rattler from which I escaped with such a narrow margin as to make me shudder at the reflection even now, some forty years after the occurrence. In the afternoon of a very hot day I entered upon pursuit of some cattle that had wandered too far from the range, and not wishing to return without them I persisted in the search until I found them and started them back at the close of the day. I drove the cattle along as hurriedly as possible, but at length the skies became overcast with heavy clouds, and in the intense darkness of the sultry night I had difficulty in finding my way. I therefore decided, as I had often done before, to halt for the night, and with the dawn overtake the cattle and proceed to the ranch headquarters. I tethered my horse so that he could graze, and, with a blanket I always carried attached to my saddle, I made my bed upon the grass, where, being very tired, I soon fell into a deep sleep. In the course of a few hours a storm gathered, and I was aroused by terrific lightning and thunder. I raised myself to a sitting posture, and in doing so I disturbed my uninvited bed-mate, a huge rattlesnake, who announced his dangerous presence with that terrifying rattle, that all who are familiar with the rattler know has but one meaning, a proclamation that he is going into action then and there. My heart stopped beating and my hair stood straight up, and I did not dare to move even if for the moment I could have done so, as I did not know the location of the snake further than to realize from the horrible rattle that he was almost against me and in easy striking distance. A vivid flash of lightning revealed his wicked snakeship just finishing his coil for the strike, and in the opposite direction I rolled with that swiftness of motion known to be quicker than sight. As I rolled I contemplated the possibility of a companion rattler on the other side, for snakes ordinarily travel in pairs. But I was spared this added peril, and after recovering some of my composure I secured my gun and dispatched what proved to be a rattler fully six feet long with eighteen rattles. I selected another resting place, and with blanket and slicker spent the remainder of the stormy night rejoicing over another escape from a grave situation. Evidently I had placed my bunk in the vicinity of the rattler, which later stretched out alongside my bed for shelter from the approaching storm. Had the snake been coiled when I sat up, he would certainly have driven his fangs into me, and with results probably fatal. As is well known, the rattler does not bite but strikes, his fangs being distended and driven in with the force of the strike; and, therefore, to strike, the snake must be coiled, enabling it to strike nearly if not quite the distance covered by its full length.

Having lived with the Indians for two years, I am in position to speak authoritatively of their inner domestic life, concerning which there has been much said and written of a fanciful and exaggerated nature. I therefore consider that in submitting certain facts along this line such will prove beneficial to all who may want to know the truth. The savage tribes subsisted mainly on buffalo meat, both fresh and dried. They also now and then partook of horse-flesh, and when it became necessary at certain intervals subsisted wholly on the meat of the horse, as at times the buffalo was not available. It was the custom to cure in the sun the meat that they would put away for winter consumption. In preparing meat they would beat it up and then parch it on the coals. Sometimes they stewed their meat, and then dipped it into a salt brine as they ate it. They had no regular hours for repasts, and had the habit of eating whenever they were hungry. They did not eat any bread at all. They lived in what is known as tepees or wigwams, which were made out of buffalo hides, dressed and tanned after a process of their own. They would take ten or fifteen buffalo skins after preparing them, and sew them together so as to make one tepee. They used the sinew of the buffalo in making thread and cord. This sinew was found in the back of the animal extending from the hip bones to the shoulder blades. It could be subdivided into small strands like thread, and each strand of the sinew had ten times the strength of the thread of the same size. They also made their bowstrings of the sinew, which strings were practically unbreakable. As before stated, the prevailing custom was for the men to have whatever number of wives or squaws they deemed neces-sary, which ordinarily amounted to two to six wives to each man. The impression has obtained that the chief

Chief Quanah Parker and His Old Home

had special prerogatives as to the number of squaws he could possess; but that is a mistake, as all the Indian men were on the same footing and permitted to have whatever number of wives they desired without respect to rank. The women that were the wives or squaws of one man all lived together and acknowledged the man as theirs in common. There were a great many more women than men, as many of the warriors were killed from time to time in their raids and battles; and owing to the greater number of women a great latitude was extended to the men as to the number of wives or squaws they should possess. Each man and his squaws would occupy tepees separately from the others, but strange to say the squaws would devote the same attention to the children of other women as they would their own. Only in rare instances was there ever any friction or discord between the squaws of the same or different households, and it was the rule, generally observed, never to whip the children, but to direct them by persuasion and object lessons. However, they were firm with their children. and commanded obedience and respect from them.

As to the manner of dress the men wore shirts, leggings, and breech clouts, and either a blanket or buffalo robe. Most of the garments were made of buckskin. They also wore moccasins on their feet, made of the same material. The Indian women and girls were dressed in buckskin, with blankets and any kind of cloth they could obtain. They would take a blanket and cut a hole in the middle so they could get their heads through, and then put a piece on each side in a V shape, so that it would spread out like a skirt and serve to drape the body. It was also a fixed custom that the squaws were to do all the menial work. They skinned and dried the buffalo meat, dressed the hides, and prepared all of the food, supplied the drinking water, moved the tepees, and in fact were the servants and menials of their lords in every manner

Comanche Babe and Cradle.

of domestic work and service. The men were always kind
and affectionate to the squaws, and were never tyrannical
in their treatment of them. Occasionally a warrior would
capture a white woman for the purpose of adding her to
his harem, and when he did so no other Indian would
dare molest him or intrude upon his exclusive ownership
of the white squaw. The women of the tribe were moral
and virtuous to a most remarkable degree, and with but
few exceptions were loyal to the men with whom they had
been mated. They seemed to have had a considerable
conception of humor, and indulged in the habit of prac-
tical jokes and much fun at each others' expense, which is
contrary to the belief so prevalent that the Indian is
stoical and solemn on all occasions.

When an Indian buck died they would kill several
horses for him to ride in the next world. They all believed implicitly in the Great Spirit, as is generally known.
They had healers known as "medicine men," and in case
of sickness or anyone being wounded the medicine men
would come and wait upon the patient in such a manner as
to call on the Great Father to help him so administer
treatment as would enable the patient to recover. In
cases of fatal illness, the grief of the parents and kinsmen
was often inconsolable. I recall one particular instance
when I was residing in Wichita Falls in 1887, when an
Indian by the name of Black Horse, in the employ of
Messrs. Frank and George Knott in Wichita Falls, who
had grass leases in the Comanche reservation, lost one of
his children. Black Horse killed five of his horses, saying
that he wanted to be sure the little boy would be well
mounted in the next world, to which he had gone. Black
Horse only had eight horses, and the killing of five left
him three only, which was not a sufficient mount for the
remaining five members of the family, and he at once
came to Wichita Falls for the purpose of having the
Knott brothers buy him two more horses. Black Horse

TAH-HAH, A Modern Comanche Indian Girl.

did not know how to explain to the Knott brothers, and he came to my home between twelve and one o'clock at night, when my family and I were sound asleep. He, however, pounded on the house and called for me by my Indian name. Finally he had aroused Mrs. Babb, who called to me, saying, "There are some Indians wanting you on the outside." Mrs. Babb was familiar with my Indian name, and for that reason understood the Indian desired to see me. I went to the door, and asked what they wanted. Black Horse related his troubles, and requested me to go with him the next morning to Mr. Knott's home and explain to him the object of his mission, as Black Horse could not speak English. I accordingly accompanied him, and after due and satisfactory explanations Mr. Knott let him have the two horses. As a further manifestation of his grief over the loss of his little boy, Black Horse had burned up his tepees, wagons, buggy, harness, and in fact most everything he had, and said he did so because in this way all of such equipment would reach his boy and be of assistance to him in the other world. I mention this instance to explain the popular conception the Indians had of death and the life hereafter.

The Indian drum or tomtom was made by stretching rawhide over some hollow vessel fashioned after the nature of a cheese hoop. The shields they used so effectively in protecting their bodies from bullets were made out of bullneck, oval shaped, about eighteen inches across, and would turn almost any bullet. These shields the Indians would use held in front if advancing, or thrown over their backs, if retreating. The Indians would undergo any amount of peril and danger in taking their wounded off the field of battle unless scalped, as they had a superstition against recovering a scalped victim of their tribe.

Chieftains were usually men who had won leadership

by personal bravery and exhibitions of courage and skill, either in the chase or on the field of battle, and where the chief proved himself worthy his descendants succeeded him in authority from one generation to another. The oldest son always took precedence in succeeding to the

An Indian Belle of recent times.

father's rank.   In the event of the death of a chief without a direct descendant to succeed him there would be held a council of the warriors who would select one of their number and install him as their chief.   There were always division chiefs, who would have direct supervision over about a thousand warriors each, and each chief would have his staff, something in the manner of a general of the army; and the chiefs and their staffs or counsellors, as they were known, were supreme in all tribal laws and regulations.   There were never any inter-tribal marriages, as the policy was for each tribe to live to itself.   They also observed much the same rules as to marrying their kin as are prescribed by the rules and laws of civilization. I have heard them explain that in this observation they desired to avoid disease, deformity, and many other ills common to intermarrying in too close a degree of kinship. They were if anything more particular in this respect than white people.   It is notable that with the Indians there is neither insanity nor epilepsy.   They had no written records of any kind and depended solely on tradition as handed down from one generation to another. They had unbounded admiration for any white man who had exhibited bravery in their combats with them, and in reviewing the past always spoke in terms of greatest praise of their white adversaries who withstood the terrible Indian charges unflinchingly.   Another striking characteristic was their truthfulness and their respect for the truth in all daily intercourse and transactions.   In the beginning they were made to undervalue the good traits of the white man, as their first contact with the white race was with thieves and outlaws, causing them to conclude that all white men were alike and that in killing and punishing them they were doing a righteous and just deed; and there can be no question but that they were more or less animated by what they esteemed to be a protection of their rights, privileges, and possessions.   The

Indian warriors generally had good discipline, and when on the warpath they would put out sentinels on high points and guard the rear as they marched or slept. Their custom was to sleep awhile and travel again, making sometimes as many as three sleeps in one night. In their skirmishes and battles the various units would sometimes become separated, and in reuniting they would at night

Present Day Indian Girls Visiting the City

build fires and surround them with blankets and thus force columns of smoke to ascend as sentinels to be seen and used as a common rendezvous.

The Indians had no eyebrows, eye lashes, nor whiskers, as they were pulled out with tweezers. The Indian men would all have whiskers about the same as white men but for this fact. The Indians were also respectful and unusually affectionate to their old people, and would provide and care for them tenderly. The Indians also in their primeval state were almost immune from disease and usually died from senility, and often attained to the great age of over a hundred years. There were rarely ever any deaths at childbirth, and the women were not very prolific, which was supposed to be due to the drudgery of their servile lives and excessive horseback riding. It would be a rare case when there would be more than three children born to one squaw. The Indian counted the winter and summer as a year each. In the burial of their dead the Comanches would select a site on a bluff and cover the remains with rocks, and in extreme cases, if a chieftain, they would dig a grave, and make interment therein. The Cheyennes buried in trees or on scaffolds. When a warrior was buried his bows, arrows, clothes, gun, and all war trappings were buried with him. The men and women were permitted to mate or marry as their mutual affections and sentiment directed, and it was a general practice of the old men to select the youngest girls whenever moved by desire to recruit their harems. Generally the Indians were very considerate of their captives, and I have known not a few to return to the Indians and others that would have returned if they had been given the opportunity. Such captives had found the Indians hospitable and generous, dividing liberally and freely any and everything they had or could get that would minister to the pleasure and comfort of the captured. Strange as it may seem, the savage tribes had

Indians drawing rations near Fort Sill

many of the instincts and finer impulses and emotions inherent in the best races of people and civilization the world over.

During my captivity with the Comanche Indians I learned their speech and lingo pretty thoroughly. Some four or five hundred words comprise their vocabulary, consisting almost wholly of nouns and adjectives. Their speech embodies mainly the names of objects. The deficiency in language as to their emotions, shades of feeling and descriptive utterances found an amplified expression in the art of gesticulation, in which they were both masterful and graceful. They had no patronymics or surnames, and derived their individual names from some closely connected circumstance, event, or happening, trivial or otherwise, and these names, even with chiefs, passed out forever with the bearer thereof.

In closing this autobiography I refrain from reciting many incidents, in the hope that I may avoid the prolixity of too voluminous a narrative. Within the scope embraced herein I have endeavored to throw some light on all of the phases of life, tribal characteristics, and viewpoints of one of the great subdivisions of the aboriginal inhabitants of North America, and in doing so I feel that I have performed no mean service. There is now left only the shadow of the multitudinous Indian tribes who until so recently overspread this continent. Before this fact can be realized the shadow will have vanished entirely and forever, and any record that will faithfully illuminate the exploits, the part played, and even the very existence of the Indian races, so numerous and powerful in the past, must enrich history and prove a valued heritage to generations now living and to follow. Being myself one of the pathfinders, I have striven to convey something of the sufferings and sacrifices of the fearless, hardy... and noble men and women who pushed ever back the borders of the frontiers and broadened the

Fourth of July Celebration, Snyder, Okla.

zone and limits of civilization.   These were the pioneers of
Texas, most of them having been called to their last
reward, but not until they realized that they had be-
queathed to mankind one of the greatest commonwealths
known to the nations of all the world.

As I now enter the lengthening shadows of life, and
looking back reckon the march of the wheels of progress,
I feel amply compensated for the privations, sorrows,
and struggles experienced and borne by me in the modest
part I have performed in that thrilling drama enacted
upon the Texas frontiers which in tragedy, endurance,
daring, pathos, variety, and intensity of action is com-
parable with the imperishable roles of the world's best
heroes in all the ages of an unmeasured past.

Present Day Comanche Mother and Son.

CPSIA information can be obtained
at www.ICGtesting.com
Printed in the USA
LVOW13s1401010517
532840LV00005B/749/P